A PRACTICAL GUIDE TO THE GREAT VEHICLE VIEW, THE TWO TRUTHS FULLY CLARIFIED

TEACHINGS OF DZA PATRUL

BY TONY DUFF
PADMA KARPO TRANSLATION COMMITTEE

Copyright © 2014 Tony Duff. All rights reserved. No portion of this book may be reproduced in any form or by any means, electronic or mechanical, including photography, recording, or by any information storage or retrieval system or technologies now known or later developed, without permission in writing from the publisher.

First edition, March 1ˢᵗ 2014
ISBN paper book: 978-9937-572-76-7
ISBN e-book: 978-9937-572-75-0

Janson typeface with diacritical marks and
Tibetan Classic typeface
Designed and created by Tony Duff
Tibetan Computer Company
http://www.pktc.org/pktc

Produced, Printed, and Published by
Padma Karpo Translation Committee
P.O. Box 4957
Kathmandu
NEPAL

Committee members for this book: translation and composition, Lama Tony Duff; editorial Jason Watkins; cover design, Christopher Duff.

Web-site and e-mail contact through:
http://www.pktc.org/pktc
or search Padma Karpo Translation Committee on the web.

CONTENTS

Introduction v

"A Practical Guide to the Great Vehicle View,
  The Two Truths Fully Clarified",
  Teachings of Dza Patrul 1

❖ ❖ ❖

Notes 17
Glossary of Terms 21
About the Author, Padma Karpo Translations
  Committee, and Their Supports for Study 41
Tibetan Text 47
Index 57

INTRODUCTION

This book contains practical instructions on the view of the two truths given according to the conventional or common Great Vehicle approach. The instructions are contained in a short text that seems to be a record of several verbal teachings by a very well-known Tibetan teacher, Jigmey Chokyi Wangpo, also known as Dza Patrul [1808–1887].

1. About Dza Patrul

Dza Patrul, meaning "the glorious tulku from Dzachuka" was born in the town of Dzachuka, which was part of the vast province that Tibetans called Kham. It is now in the very north of the modern-day Szechuan province of China. Dzachuka has been a hive of Buddhist activity for a number of centuries and is home to many monasteries and retreat hermitages, especially of the Kagyu and Nyingma traditions of the Buddhist teaching.

Dza Patrul grew up in Dzachuka as a Kagyu follower. He became expert in the sūtras and tantras and a very capable meditator as well. As a young man, he heard of the teachings of Jigmey Lingpa, who had received the complete transmission of the most profound level of Great Completion (Dzogchen) teachings in a series of direct mind contacts with the earlier great holder of those teachings, Longchen Rabjam. The teachings of this transmission had become known as Longchen Nyingthig or the Quintessence Teaching of Longchen Rabjam. Dza Patrul wanted these teachings, so he went off to study with the main disciples of Jigmey Lingpa. After receiving all of the teachings and transmissions of Longchen Nyingthig, Dza Patrul made his way to Dzogchen Monastery, which by that time had become a hub of the Longchen Nyingthig teaching. Patrul lived there for the remainder of his life, spending most of his time in retreat with his disciples, developing his realization of the Great Completion teachings he had received and teaching them to his disciples. Due to his unrelenting efforts Dza Patrul gained an enormous understanding of dharma, both sūtra and tantra, and high realization of the Nyingthig or Quintessence Great Completion teachings to go with it.

Figure 1. Dza Patrul

His name Patrul means "glorious tulku" and he explained that his name was due to having the glory of extreme expertise in the sūtras and tantras. He used several pen-names in his writings, the most well known of which—"The Glorious Expert King"—also indicated that he was a king amongst practitioners, glorious with expertise in the sūtras and tantras.

2. About Dza Patrul's Text

After Dza Patrul died, his own writings and also notes of his teachings that had been recorded by his disciples were collected and published as the *Collected Works of Orgyan Jigmey Chokyi Wangpo* in a total of five Tibetan volumes. The wood blocks were cut and the work was published at the nearby Derge Printery.

The texts contained in his *Collected Works* tend not to be highly polished compositions and the production as a whole has more than the usual number of typographic errors. This reflects the fact that he was a yogi for most of his life, living in the very high and rugged mountains that are home to Dzogchen monastery, and also that the producers of his *Collected Works* would have been the yogis who lived with him. Polished compositions and polished productions tend to happen within large institutions, not in caves.

Many of the "texts" contained in his *Collected Works* are more like notes that he wrote himself or which his disciples recorded from his oral teachings. Some of them superficially seem to be a "text" composed by Patrul himself but are in fact several teachings on a certain subject that his disciples brought together into one text for inclusion into the *Collected Works*[1], and

---

[1] It is usual when a teacher dies to collect all of his writings, notes of his teachings, letters written to friends and disciples containing teachings, and so on, for inclusion into a published set of the teacher's collected works. It is also usual for the compilers to put smaller bits and pieces of teachings heard, the teacher's own (continued...)

the text here is one of them. The text here starts with a complete but short teaching on the two truths and is completed with several fragments of teaching that enhance that teaching. These various segments of teaching are shown in the Tibetan text by the use of a special punctuation mark and are likewise shown in the translation here by the use of an ornamental section mark.

2.1. The Text Presents the Non-Dual Teaching of the Two Truths in General and the Great Completion Teaching of the two truths in Particular

Despite Dza Patrul's great mastery of the Quintessence Great Completion teaching, only one of the five volumes of his *Collected Works* is dedicated to it. The remaining four volumes are taken up with explanations of conventional Great Vehicle theory and practice. The text here is from one of those four volumes and contains, as its title says, instructions on the view and practice of the two truths according to the conventional Great Vehicle.

In the text, Dza Patrul starts by presenting the two truths according to the conventional presentation of the subject that is found in the sūtras, but goes on to connect it to the non-dual wisdom teachings of the third sūtra turning of the wheel and then to the Quintessence Great Completion teachings which are the ultimate non-dual teaching of the two truths.

---

[1](...continued)

writings, and so on into a single text which they then name appropriately. The result of the latter can easily look as though the text was written and titled by the teacher himself when that is not the case and that is what has happened here.

Key Great Completion terms such as "rigpa", "crossing over", "appearances of the liveliness", and so on begin to appear as the text progresses and are telltale markers of the gradual shift to a Great Completion approach to the two truths. The final section of the text teaches the two truths using a direct presentation of the Thorough Cut teaching of Quintessence Great Completion. This has been done skilfully to show that, in the end, the practice of the two truths is none other than the practice of the Thorough Cut of Great Completion.

The overall emphasis on the non-dual view of the two truths coupled with the final presentation of the two truths as the practice of Great Completion makes the text very interesting for practitioners in general and for Great Completion practitioners in particular.

2.2. The Text Combines View and Practice

The wording of the title conveys the type of teaching present in the text. The Tibetan term "lta khrid" in the title translates literally as "guidance to the view". However, it immediately signifies to a Tibetan reader that the text consists of practical instructions on the matter, so this part of the title has been correctly translated as "a practical guide to the view".[2]

---

[2] There is another translation of this text into English available through a place called "Lotsawa House" on the internet. Unfortunately the translator seems not to have understood many aspects of the text and the teaching in it. For example, he mistakenly presents the text as though it is a single text all written by Dza Patrul. In regard to that he has deliberately removed all of the division markers that show the text to be a composite of various teachings and even gone so far as to add the words (continued...)

Rather than being another one of the very dry presentations of the view of the two truths that have appeared in Tibetan literature—such as in the literature of the scholarly Gelugpa tradition—this text presents both the view of the two truths and the practice needed to realize them.

3. The Topic of the Text: The Two Truths

The Buddha taught what he called "the two truths" in order to give his followers a survey of the various realities that beings live in. The first truth is called "fictional truth" and the second is called "superfactual truth".

What does "truth" mean here? Firstly, it is a very accurate rendering of the original Sanskrit term "satya", which literally means a truth or that which is true. In this specific context it means a kind of reality which the being experiencing that reality believes to be true. For example, a person who sees a mirage of water and who does not know about mirages usually believes, at least for a while, that there is water ahead. It is unquestionably true for that person that there is water ahead. That person's reality or what is true for him at that time includes water ahead. That is the sense of "truth" in the two truths.

---

[2](...continued)

"Written by Patrul Rinpoche" to the end of the text when there is no such ending because that is not the case. Moreover, this translation exhibits a lack of knowledge of many of the details involved in this subject and present in the text, and ends up being a translation which, although it reads smoothly, both loses and mistakenly presents much of the meaning of the original.

The Buddha understood that, if you were to describe the various truths or realities that beings experience, you would need to mention exactly two types of truth or reality. You would have to mention one which was, no matter how true it seemed to the person experiencing it, a fiction. The example above makes it very easy to understand the use of the word "fiction" in relation to the term "truth". It is understood in our world that humans experience many realities which are known to be fictions invented by the mind of the person experiencing them and, in the Sanskrit-speaking culture of the Buddha's time, the Tibetan-speaking culture following it, and also in English-speaking cultures, the word "fiction" is precisely the term used to discuss this sort of truth or reality.

The Buddha understood that you would also need to mention a superior kind of truth, one that was not fictional but completely factual; one so factual that it could not be argued with. In the Buddha's time and even now, various Indian religions had and have a word for this superior and ultimate kind of factual truth or reality. Thus, for this second kind of truth, the Buddha simply used the term that was in common use within the religious and philosophical systems of the time. The term literally is "superfactual truth". The actual superfact pointed to by the term is the ultimate destination for his followers.

In short, the Buddha taught fictional truth to show his followers the false or fictional realities that occur to them in their un-enlightened existence and taught superfactual truth to show them the superior and factual reality lived in by enlightened beings.

The path from an ordinary, mundane type of existence with its fictional realities to the complete enlightenment of a buddha with its purely superfactual reality proceeds in stages as the shrouds that cover mind are gradually removed. Because of this there are many degrees of fictional reality, corresponding to the degrees of removal of the shrouds of mind that cause the fictions to appear. Nevertheless, the Buddha reduced them to two: incorrect and correct fictional truths.

It is common for those just learning the two truths to equate fictional truth with appearance and superfactual truth with emptiness. However, in the end, it is more subtle than that because the two truths in the end must be unified or non-dual.

When equating fictional truth with appearance, the fiction involved can be divided into correct and incorrect fiction. Correct fictional truth is fictional truth that is the norm and incorrect fictional truth is a mistaken take on that. For example, a person with severe Hepatitis has their eyes go yellow and because of that sees yellow where people without the disease see white. Both the white and yellow colours are fictions but the white appearance is at least correct for people operating normally within their agreed-on fiction whereas the yellow appearance is incorrect. This sort of presentation of correct and incorrect fictional is the one that many people learn.

There is another level of correct and incorrect fictional which comes in connection with a non-dual understanding of the two truths. In it, the fictional truth of ordinary beings—meaning those who have not advanced spiritually—is an incorrect version of fictional truth. And, the fictional truth of noble beings—meaning those who have advanced spiritually to the point of having gained direct sight of emptiness—is a correct version of fictional truth.

There is yet another level, which is the fictional truth of fictional truth and superfactual truth unified. That level of the two truths is the ultimate two truths known only by a buddha and in it there is no correct and incorrect fictional truth.

The above brief explanation of the differing ways of proclaiming fictional truth will help clarify Patrul's presentation of the same.

The basic idea of the two truths as presented above is not hard to understand. However, the two truths have been taught in various ways in accordance with the various levels of the Buddha's teaching, with the result that there can be confusion over what the two truths actually mean. Unravelling that confusion can be difficult because it requires detailed dissections of the various levels of profound teachings that the Buddha gave concerning reality. Thus, it would be easy to take Dza Patrul's text here and write a very long commentary on its first section alone, a section which stays mainly within standard sūtra presentations. A much longer commentary again could be written to the entire text, which would delve into all the levels of the two truths, ending with the most profound view and practice of Great Completion's Thorough Cut as the final view and practice of the two truths.

4. A Major Problem with Terminology

I presented above, without flinching or excuses, the names of the two truths as "fictional" and "superfactual" respectively. Some readers will wonder about this because they will only have heard "relative" and "absolute" (or sometimes these days "ultimate") as the names of the two truths. Without any apologies, I am stating here that "relative and absolute" are not just minor mistakes of translation but are major mistakes that simply cannot be justified. Worse—and it is a very real problem—these mistaken translations "relative" and "absolute" take the person using them in a completely wrong direction, giving them an understanding which is totally at variance with what the Buddha and all the other religious figures of India intended! Note that the glossary in this book contains further explanations of the terms fictional and superfactual and why they are not only the correct translations of the original terms used by the Buddha but very exact translations of those original terms.

It is tempting to write a very long dissertation here of why "relative and absolute" are not merely wrong but why their use creates a barrier to correctly understanding the Buddha's teaching whereas the terms "fictional and superfactual" are not only correct but open the door to a correct understanding of the same. However, and most unfortunately, I have discovered that there is a willful blindness concerning these terms, at least amongst my generation of Buddhists. Some people in this group say that they have no knowledge about the details of these terms and where they come from, but that they have been using "relative and absolute" for many years, so the two terms must be correct. That is, of course, no valid reason at all for them to be correct. Some others say that their Tibetan teachers always use the terms "relative and absolute" so they must be correct. In fact, various Tibetan teachers have gone on record over the last several years, saying that "relative and absolute" bear no resemblance to the meaning of the Tibetan terms and that they should be replaced with better translations. For example, the very well-known Lama Zopa of the FPMT made similar comments some years ago, then pointed out that "fictional" was a good fit, and so on. Others in this group come up with various other arguments all of which come down to a total lack of knowledge of the matter and total unwillingness to give up clinging to their cherished ideas.

4.1. The Meaning of the Original Sanskrit Terms for the Two Truths

The original Sanskrit terms for the two truths are "saṃvṛtti satya" and "paramārtha satya" respectively. The "satya" in each means "truth" or "reality" as explained above. There is no great disagreement over the meaning of this term, so we will not look at it further, but will focus on the two terms "saṃvṛtti" and "paramārtha".

It has to be noted that the Tibetans literally and perfectly translated these terms into Tibetan. For the Tibetans who know the grammar and etymology involved, there is no disagreement at all over the meaning of the terms as they appear in Tibetan. They understand the terms in exactly the same way as the Indians did.

To understand the meaning of the two terms as they appear in both Sanskrit and Tibetan, I first heard large amounts of teaching on the two truths and related matters from many of the best Tibetan teachers of my time. Having heard their teachings, it was clear to me that "relative and absolute" were just mistaken and bore no resemblance at all to the original terms. For example, the late Khenpo Palden Sherab, a Nyingma master well known in the United States for his exceptional scholarship gave a long dissertation in the 1980's on the meaning of these terms to a meeting of the Nālandā Translation Committee of which I was a member. His explanations in Tibetan convinced me that my doubts about the only translations in use at the time, "relative and absolute", were correct. Moreover, his explanations matched exactly with those of the Sanskrit experts whom I later consulted, as explained next.

In order to be certain of the meaning of the original Sanskrit terms, I went to a number of Sanskrit experts in India, and especially to the Sanskrit professor of the Tibetan University of Higher Studies in Sarnath, near Varanasi, the city which these days is the home of the Brahmin scholars and practitioners who hold and even still speak the Sanskrit language. It is noteworthy that the discussions did not go on for long with any of these Sanskrit experts because, as they said, there was no argument or disagreement whatsoever about the meaning of the terms "saṃvṛtti" and "paramārtha" amongst Indians. They explained that the first term is an everyday term and the second a religious or philosophical term.

According to them, the term "saṃvṛtti" unequivocally means "fiction", "a lie", "a deliberate cover-up", "a hoax". Moreover, of all the words in English that could be used to translate it, such as "lie", "falsehood", "dissimulation", "concealment", the one that they always said was the right choice was "fiction" and from that "fictional". They pointed out, moreover, that there were other words in Sanskrit that exactly matched the other possibilities such as "lie", "falsehood", and so on, so those would not be fitting translations. In short, there was just no question about this in the minds of these experts who were fluent in both Sanskrit and English, and who also were practising Hindus with an enormous knowledge of how these terms were used in their own and the Buddhist religions.

The original Sanskrit term for the second truth, "paramārtha", is a philosophical term used by several Indian religions to indicate the higher spiritual truth of their systems. "Parama" is an adjective meaning something which is superior, better, higher, and is also used to mean "holy". "Artha" can have a number of meanings, an important one of which is "meaning". In this case, "artha" means a fact for mind, not in the sense of a conceptually known fact, but simply the fact or datum which registers on the mind.

The Sanskrit scholars informed me that "paramārtha" is the term commonly used in many Indian religions to indicate the highest truth for the religion. They pointed out and I have seen myself in Buddhist explanations that using a translation like "highest truth" which goes easily into English will not work for the simple fact that each part of the original term is given a very precise meaning, which can be commented on at length, and those parts must be retained in the translation. In other words, the translation must not only correctly convey the meaning of the term overall but must also be etymologically correct and complete. Therefore, I have done exactly what the Tibetans did and have created a new word in English that conveys the sense of the term while maintaining its etymology. The base meaning of "parama" is "a superior kind of", so I have used "super" for that and "artha" means "fact" so I have used "fact" for that. The result is the new word "superfact" or "superfactual" when used as an adjective. It would take a chapter to go through why this is such a good rendition of the original term. However, in sum, the term overall captures the sense of the highest kind of truth as well as the necessary sense of it being factual as opposed to fictional and the etymology of the new word matches the etymology of the original term exactly, which means that all deep explanations of the meaning of the term found in Tibetan Buddhist literature can be translated exactly.

How could any Westerner disagree with the greatest experts of both Tibetan and Sanskrit languages without being thoroughly dishonest?! Unfortunately, I have found that they do, so it is necessary to belabour the point.

Other translators in particular should pay attention to all of the above; it is a singularly important issue. Non-translators should not brush it off because of habits of using terms like "relative" and "absolute". I urge people of both groups to pick up and read a Buddhist text that uses the words "relative" and "absolute" for the two truths. As you read, exchange "fictional" for "relative" and "superfactual" for "absolute" and see what happens. I am sure, based on my own experience and the experiences of those who have done it, that you will discover a whole new world of meaning that was not being conveyed to you with those incorrect terms. It is very important to understand that the new world of meaning that you will discover in doing so is the actual meaning that has been in Buddhist teaching and treatises on it from the time the Buddha first spoke about it.

5. More About the Two Truths

The first half of the text of Patrul's teachings on the two truths concerns itself with the meaning of the two truths. In short, "fictional truth" is what is true for a consciousness which is dealing in the fictions of dualistic appearances that it throws up for you to mistakenly believe. "Superfactual truth" is what is true for a non-dualistic mind seeing what actually is, which in a conventional way of talking is the highest truth possible, a super or superior kind of truth.

5.1. Two Truths Exactly

Why two truths? Why not one or three or more truths? The Buddha himself answered this question. He said in a sūtra that one truth, although it would encompass all truths of realities for all minds, was not sufficient to explain the entire situation of reality to confused sentient beings. Firstly, their fictional and unsatisfactory reality needed to be explained and then, secondly, their super (factual) truth or, as he also called it, their "authentic or true reality" also needed to be explained. Thus, he said that not one but two truths had to be explained. He went on to say that three or more truths would contain the two truths and nothing more than further subdivisions of them. Therefore, he said, three or more truths were more than needed. He concluded by saying that two truths is the exact count of how many truths need to be presented so that his followers can understand what they need to understand and then be able to practice accordingly.

5.2. Fictional Truth?

Some people have tried to argue that "fictional" cannot be correct because "fictional truth" is an oxymoron. How can a "fiction" be "true", they demand? When this question is answered, it serves to show that the apparent contradiction in terms is exactly what the Buddha intended, confirming that "fictional" is the correct term to use. The whole point is that some realities are fictions but are taken to be true by the minds projecting those realities. "Fictional truth" is exactly what the Buddha intended; he was using it to show that all beings who have not become enlightened buddhas are stuck in realities of their own making which are cover-ups. Those fictional realities have the unfortunate consequence of being the basis for creating the causes for more fictional realities, all of which are unsatisfactory in one way or another.

5.3. Superfactual Truth

Superfactual truth is a name for the highest kind of reality; the reality which is true, authentic, and so on because it is what is without any distortion or cover-up. Ordinary beings do not contact that reality, even though they are, in fact, immersed in it. Bodhisatvas—the ones who are on the way to complete enlightenment—who have reached the bodhisatva levels see superfact in their formal meditation but not in their post-meditation. Buddhas, those who are fully enlightened, see superfact all of the time.

Superfact is the state of being in which the completely purified mind of enlightenment has none of the cover-ups that previously prevented it from seeing that superfact in full, unhindered view. The concepts of dualistic mind are like little things that suddenly pop up in vast enlightened mind and, in doing so, prevent that mind from seeing superfact. Therefore, superfact is finally described as the total absence of all elaborated conceptual structures. That freedom from elaboration is at the same time a completely uninhibited view of what actually is. That is the Thorough Cut way of describing the unified two truths.

Each level of the Buddha's teaching has its own way of presenting the two truths. Thus, as mentioned earlier, it would be possible to continue on from the above short explanation and what Dza Patrul says in his short teachings to give a vast explanation of the two truths and the meditations used to realize them. Unfortunately, there is not time to do that here. However, the ultimate presentation of the two truths in the sūtra tradition is found in the Other Emptiness teachings of the third turning of the wheel and in the tantric tradition is found in the explanations and transmissions of both Essence Mahāmudrā and Quintessence Great Completion and we have published many texts to clarify these various teachings for the reader.

With my best wishes,
Tony Duff,
Padma Karpo Translation Committee,
Swayambunath,
Nepal,
February 2014

A PRACTICAL GUIDE TO THE GREAT VEHICLE VIEW THE TWO TRUTHS FULLY CLARIFIED
A Text of Teachings by Dza Patrul

This clarification of the two truths has two main topics: the dharma that is to be realized by those wanting emancipation and the dharma that they will practise in order to realize it.

I. The Dharma to be Realized

This has two parts: the actuality of knowables in general and the actuality of their knower itself.

I.I. The Actuality of Knowables in General

This has two parts: the fictional and the superfactual.

I.I.I. The Fictional
Generally speaking, all appearances from those of the lowest hell of Avichi up to and including those of the post-meditation experience of bodhisatvas[1] on the tenth level are the fictional.

Moreover, those fictional appearances are of two types, incorrect and correct fictional, as follows. Starting with beginners, the whole extent of their appearance is the incorrect fictional. Going up a step, for those at the level of intentional conduct[2], at the time when they are considered to have comprehension, all appearance is correct fictional and when not, all of it is incorrect fictional. Going up further still, for those who have attained the levels, the whole extent of what appears to mental mind is correct fictional—being mere appearance that does not stop it is the fictional and it is seen in direct perception to be false[3]. Now those appearances of the first to tenth levels are produced because the latencies of the very long term habit of grasping at things[4] in the past have not yet been eliminated; they are similar to the way that the scent of musk lingers in a container. Having completely eliminated those latencies, the buddhas never have those appearances, remaining exclusively in freedom from elaboration in the superfactual.

Clinging to the things in the ordinary outer environments and beings in them is the incorrect fictional. The antidotes to that of transforming the environments and beings into purity's illusion-like deities and immeasurable palaces then meditating on them[5], and so on, are the correct fictional.

1.1.2. The Superfactual

The entity of the superfactual—the superfactual itself—is the dharmadhātu free of elaboration. There is no making of divisions in the entity itself, but if we divide it up according to the aspects of its having been made manifest or not, there is the superfact which is one's own nature, one's innate disposition, and there is the superfact produced by having manifested the realization of that nature. Alternatively, there is the superfact understood through cutting overstatements of it with hearing and contemplation and there is the one directly experienced by a yogin. Or, there is the superfact of individualized beings which is a generic image obtained through inference and there is the one of noble ones known by them in self-knowing direct perception. Moreover, those have been taught as "assessed and unassessed superfact".

Those Two Truths Have Three Modes of Appearance

That set of two truths has three modes of appearance. Appearance that appears to one's own mindstream and does so together with clinging is the individualized beings' level, referred to as "the incorrect fictional". Appearance that is realized to be false and is not clung to is the noble ones' level, called "the correct fictional". Being without any appearance or non-appearance whatsoever and free of considering whether there is clinging or not is the buddhas' level, and that exactly is called "the superfactual".

In other words, in the first case there is both appearance and clinging, in the second case there is mere appearance due to which there is no clinging, and in the last case there is neither appearance nor clinging.

Those three also are known as "an awareness which is incorrect", "an awareness which knows the fictional", and "an awareness which knows superfact".

Individualized beings' prajñā awareness that knows the fictional is dependent on analysis; noble ones know the fictional in direct perception.

The superfact dharmadhātu does not have in it the conventions of knowing and not knowing, nevertheless the full internal comprehension of it is named "understanding", "realization", and so on.

The ultimate two truths will be realized as an indivisible two truths and for that a designation of "the fictional" as existence and "the superfactual" as the non-existence would not be the view of the Middle Way. When the one real correct fictional is realized, right at that time those separate two truths merge into an indivisible two truths free of all extremes of existence and non-existence, permanence and annihilation. As it says in the *Mother*:[6]

> What is the nature of the fictional itself is the nature of the superfactual.

The division into two truths is, moreover, simply a designation made in relation to the two aspects in order to facilitate understanding for the time being. It designates the appearance of various things to a confused awareness as "fiction" and designates the absence of referencing of so much as a speck of anything at all, including even the absence of it, in an awareness for which the confusion has been ended as "superfact". That has been said like this[7]:

> When things and non-things
> Are not present before rational mind,
> There are at that time no other superficies, so
> Without referencing[8], they are utterly pacified.

In fact—meaning in the innate disposition of knowables—the ultimate dharmadhātu which is the great freedom from elaboration, there is no basis of designation for the divided two truths, so there is no division that could be made. And, for the mind of someone who has gone to the ultimate, a buddha, there also is no division into two truths that could be made. Even this confused appearance that we have now is not present as two separate, different truths; it resides as inseparable appearance-emptiness, as inseparable knowing-emptiness, and exactly the realization or full internal comprehension of it as such is the mind of a buddha, the wisdom of non-dual dharmatā. Correctly knowing each part of the two truths and having the two merged indivisible is named "unification non-dual wisdom", "non-dwelling nirvana", and so on.[9]

1.2. The Actuality of the Knower Itself

The actuality of the object—knowables in general—might be realized in that way, but if the actuality of the subject—the knower itself—is not realized, then all phenomena will be left at being knowable objects. As a result, that realization will not become an antidote to the afflictions, but instead will give rise to arrogance and conceit[10] and will only strengthen the sense of a personal self. Thus, the actuality of the rational mind or mind or mental mind or consciousness that is the knower of the knowables must itself be realized.

Now, there are two aspects to this: the provisional realization that has to be made of two truths and the ultimate realization that has to be made of indivisible truths.

1.2.1. The Provisional Realization

The rational mind or the awareness that realizes that the actuality of the fictional appearances of knowables in general is that they are without nature, illusion-like, that realizes that in superfact they, being not at all established as existing and not existing, are space-like, and that realizes them as the Great Middle Way which is the ultimate indivisible two truths, the dharmadhātu free of all elaborations of limits and extremes, is the fictional. As Shāntideva said[11]:

> The superfactual is not the domain of rational mind.
> We assert that rational mind is the fictional.

The rational mind that realizes in that way has arrogance and conceit and, given that arrogance and conceit is the work of māra, that mind itself is understood to be a wrong awareness. As *The Sūtra Showing the Inconceivable Domain of the Buddhas* says:

> So-called "attainment" is unsteadiness. So-called "manifest realization" is conceit. That unsteadiness and conceit is the work of māra. Those with a higher level of arrogance will have the discursive thoughts "I have attained!" and "I have produced a manifest realization".

This nature of this fictional rational mind that realizes is superfact. By looking at that rational mind or mind or awareness itself, we find that it is not established as a thing at all. It is primordially empty of existence and non-existence, empty of arising and ceasing, empty of coming and going, empty of permanence and annihilation, empty of the three times, so it is called "the superfactual dharmatā".

The Sūtra Petitioned by Kāshyapa says:

> Mind does not exist inside nor does it exist outside and it is not referenced as not both.

The Sūtra Petitioned by Maitreya says:
> Mind has no shape, has no colour, has no location; it is like space.

1.2.2. The Ultimate Realization

The actuality of the mind resides as the ultimate indivisible two truths; even designation of the one mindness as the two truths simply ends up being merely a name, merely a symbol for communication, merely a conceptual understanding, all of which is provisonal and partial understanding only. In the ground dharmadhātu there is no mind, so there is no basis for the designation "two truths". In the fruition buddha mind there is no mind, so there can be no designating of two truths. Moreover, in this luminous-empty mindness of confused sentient beings there is no identification, so it is by staying in luminous-empty rigpa that the indivisible two truths are to be realized[12]. Nevertheless, the realization of the fact of the indivisible two truths requires knowledge of the two truth's characteristics, because of which the fact of it is divided into two aspects.

In that way, both the elaboration-free actuality of knowables and the elaboration-free actuality of the knower are merged into one taste, indivisible. Its mere emptiness of phenomena having being freed of all elaborations of existence and non-existence and permanence and annihilation, it is realized and seen in a manner which is without seer and seen, without realizer and realized, to be like uncompounded space, which is its un-mistaken realization.

2. The Dharma that will be Practised

This has two parts: the immediate-style practice for those with sharp faculties and the gradual-style practice for those of duller faculties.

2.1. The Immediate-Style Practice for Those with Sharp Faculties

Those who have the good fortune of a profound karmic connection with the two truths, who have the cause of having gathered the two accumulations in the past, will have its realization shine forth simply by being instructed in it and then all they need to do is to preserve that state of realization. They will meditate in an equipoise empty of both knower and knowables and without a self, in a state which, free of the elaborations of two truths, is space-like. When they are doing that sort of meditation, they will not be getting rid of bad discursive thought and not be entrusting themselves to a good type of mind. As Guardian Maitreya said:[13]

> In this there is nothing at all to be removed,
> Not the slightest thing to be added.
> One authentically looks at the authentic itself;
> If the authentic is seen, there is complete liberation.

In post-meditation, all appearances whatever they are like appear without a nature, so they preserve the unified two truths in a dream-like state. For the sake of dream-like, illusion-like sentient beings who have not realized that, they will utilize the merely illusory enlightenment mind of loving-kindness and compassion to accumulate the merely illusory two accumulations and will make vast prayers of aspiration for the sake of those sentient beings.

2.2. The Gradual-Style Practice for Those with Duller Faculties

Those with duller faculties have to familiarize themselves gradually, starting with the four mind-reversers[14]. If they do not, profound realization will not arise except as a mere generic image of the same.

The Summation in Verse

> All appearances of thought, whatever they are like,
>   are the fictional;
> Their nature realized is superfact.
> The rational mind which realizes such is fictional;
> Rational mind being without a nature is superfact.
> The sounds expressing the two truths are fictional;
> Sounds being without a nature is superfact.
> The non-duality of those is the two truths unified;
> In the innate disposition of the knowable and the
>   buddha mind
> The unity of the two truths is not even referenced,
> So that, the dharmadhātu, is called "free from
>   elaboration".
> In it, the selves of persons and phenomena do not
>   exist.
> That sort of realization is the view;
> Remaining in its state is the meditation;
> Gathering the accumulations out of compassion for
>   the sake of others is the conduct;
> The vanishing of grasped-grasping into the dhātu is
>   the fruition;

> Wisdom pervading everywhere without partiality is the good qualities;
> And the automatic meaningful accomplishment that proceeds from that is the enlightened activity.
> Rather than grasping at the words and symbols of communication as the actual fact,
> Turn your mind to the fact which the words and symbols point towards.

The agent producing the appearance, mindness, is without a nature, so it was designated as being "without self, without sentient being, without person, without agent", and so on[15]. The term "without" used in that has the final meaning "does not exist". Because of that "does not exist", it is said "also does not not exist". All together, those words stand for the words "no establishment in it anywhere of existent and non-existent".

It has been taught: "This consciousness that knows its object does not depend on the sense faculties, does not originate from its object, and does not reside in between the two. It is not inside; it is not outside. When it arises it does not come from anywhere; when it ceases it does not go anywhere. It arises yet is empty; it disintegrates yet is empty …"

A sutra says:

> In that seeing of the authentic, no phenomena at all will appear.

The *Mother* says:

> That mentation will cause involvement with the desire realm, the form realm, and the formless realm, whereas not mentating will not cause involvement with any of them.

A sutra says:

> When one does not do any activity ever,
> It is therefore called "yoga activity"[16].

And:

> To preserve what is ordinary in a dharma-less state, is the supreme dharma.

A sutra says:

> Where is there supreme dharma in that?
> Where there is no perception of dharmas.

The *Mother* says:

> Because enlightenment is without referencing, this so-called "enlightenment" is no more than a mere name. Buddhahood being without referencing is no more than a mere name.

The realization that in the space-like actuality of all dharmas there can be no becoming an object of consciousness or of wisdom is the view. The residing in that state in the manner of not residing is the meditation. The illusion-like gathering in post-meditation of an accumulation of merit for the sake of the merely illusory sentient beings is the conduct. That the merely illusory rational mind appears but vanishes into the dhātu is the final fruition.

> For the dharmadhātu free of elaboration, beyond expressions of speech and thought,
> Even the knower itself that knows the objects of the knowable does not exist.
> Doing, while there is this non-existence, the practise of its view and meditation
> Is nothing more than space practising view and meditation of space.

> In the fact of the authentic there is no mind, there is no appearance,
> And even the non-existence of it is absent,
> So it is beyond the considerations of existence and non-existence.

It is explained that not being afraid of the fact of profound emptiness and that being glad at the idea of residing in it and intending to so is the mark of a person who possesses the good fortune of having heard and trained in its teaching in the past as well and who will quickly attain enlightenment.

The space-like dharmatā whose dhātu cannot be known with mind;
The state of inexpressible wisdom realizing that;
The consideration-less, activity-free, innate nature, equality;
This is the mind of the buddhas of the three times.

In superfact dharmatā, which is like the son of a barren woman,
The un-manifest, unthought of, ordinary innate's state;
The fictional dharmins, unification's illusions,[17]
Not accepted, not rejected, without clinging are used,
Which is the practice of gaining experience in the buddha mind.

For as long as mastery over the mind has not been gained,
Being without attachment to all material possessions
And keeping to remote forest areas like the peaceful forest creatures,
One stays on the non-reversing path.

Not hindered by having like and dislike, attachment and aversion towards

Any of the circumstances, outer and inner,
   favourable and unfavourable,
And having the greatness of whatever occurs being a
   helper on the path,
One achieves finality in the unborn dharma.

Both the prajñā realizing space-like mindness and
The compassion which does not abandon illusory
   sentient beings
Are brought into unification to provide the view and
   then having conduct consistent with that
The great non-abiding wisdom will be quickly
   attained.

The *Nirvāṇa Sutra* says:

> To be empty is not to see the two, empty and not empty. The self-complexion of that being empty can appear as anything at all and right upon appearing it is empty, so there is unified appearance and emptiness. Exactly that can only be known by oneself turning inwards and knowing it, nothing other than that, so is referred to as "the domain of personal, self-knowing wisdom".

Machig said:

> If you have not engaged in any mentation,
> How could you possibly go astray?
> Put yourself into letting perceptions disintegrate
>   completely.

and:

> In mind there is no duality, so
> Look at it in the manner of there being no looking
>   to be done.
> Having looked you do not see your own mind.
> That being so, in terms of what is to be looked at
> There is not a speck of it at all.

It has been said:

> Mindness, empty luminosity without referencing, is the true actuality of the innate disposition. Exactly that elaboration-free and identification-less rigpa has appearances of its liveliness shining forth non-stop in an illusion-like way, so you cross over to the state of indivisible or unified equipoise and post-meditation, luminosity-emptiness without grasping, then practice to gain experience in that.

NOTES

1. See bodhisatva in the glossary for notes on its correct spelling.

2. For intentional conduct, see the glossary.

3. The second half of this sentence answers the question "Why is it correct fictional?" Firstly, for these beings on the levels it is mere dream-like appearance. Mere in this case means that do not cling strongly to it, understanding that it is merely an appearance and no more. However, it still is occurring for them without interruption, because the latencies for it have not been stopped. Thus, it remains appearance of the fictional sort. Nevertheless, they see it in direct perception to be false. Therefore, because it is known in direct perception to be what it is—false—it is the correct fictional.

4. It is important to note that "things" throughout this text has the specific meaning of "things which are a product of conceptual or dualistic mind".

5. This first antidote mentioned refers to the practice of the development stage of a deity. There is a point here. Those practices, which are often mistakenly thought to be final practices, are still only fictional truths, although within that they are correct fictional truths. The mere visualization of

oneself as a deity and the external world as the deity's palace is still not at the level of superfact.

6. "The *Mother*" means the *Prajñāpāramitā* sutras.

7. ... in Shāntideva's *Entering the Bodhisatva's Conduct* IX.34, the chapter which presents Shāntideva's understanding of the Middle Way and necessarily deals with the meaning of the two truths ...

8. Here and elsewhere the phrase "without referencing" specifically means being completely without dualistic mind because of being without the referencing process which dualistic mind uses to know through concepts.

9. This sentence presents the ultimate experience of the two truths. In it, each of the two truths is known precisely and without mixup. However, time, the two aspects are merged inseparable. This is how the two truths are known by a buddha's wisdom.

10. ... where conceit specifically means pride over having some spiritual development, such as this realization ...

11. ... in Shāntideva's *Entering the Bodhisatva's Conduct* IX.2, the chapter which presents Shāntideva's understanding of the Middle Way and necessarily deals with the meaning of the two truths ...

12. The ground is the luminous-empty mindness that is innate to all beings with a mind. The path to that is the practice of rigpa, which is the actual fact of that luminosity and emptiness as experienced by the practitioner.

13. ... in Maitreya-Asaṅga's *Highest Continuum* I.154 ...

14. These are often called "mind-changers" but the actual term is "mind reversers" which is given to them because they do not merely change the mind but reverse it so that it is now headed in the opposite direction from saṃsāra. The four mind reversers are the contemplations on: precious human rebirth, impermanence and death, karmic cause and effect, and the disadvantages of saṃsāra.

15. These seemingly strange descriptions of emptiness were taught by the Buddha. More can be read about them in the PKTC publication *Maitreya's Sutras and Prayer with Commentary by Padma Karpo,* by Tony Duff and Tamás Agócs, 2013, ISBN 978-9937-572-62-0.

16. This refers to the Yogāchāra system of teachings found in the third turning of the wheel. What is a person who is "yogāchāra", that is, actually doing the practice of joining with superfact? It is a person who has ended dualistic phenomena.

17. Fictional dharmins are the conceived of dharmas or phenomena that appear to someone who has not accomplished the path. Unification illusions means that although they appear to that person's mind as fictional dharmas, they are in fact the illusory appearances within the superfact of the unified two truths.

GLOSSARY OF TERMS

Actuality, Tib. gnas lugs: A key term in both sūtra and tantra and one of a pair of terms, the other being "apparent reality" (Tib. snang lugs). The two terms are used when determining the reality of a situation. The actuality of any given situation is how (lugs) the situation actuality sits or is present (gnas); the apparent reality is how (lugs) any given situation appears (snang) to an observer. Something could appear in many different ways, depending on the circumstances at the time and on the being perceiving it but, regardless of those circumstances, it will always have its own actuality of how it really is.

Affliction, Skt. kleśha, Tib. nyon mongs: This term is usually translated as emotion or disturbing emotion, etcetera, but the Buddha was very specific about the meaning of this word. When the Buddha referred to the emotions, meaning a movement of mind, he did not refer to them as such but called them "kleśha" in Sanskrit, meaning exactly "affliction". It is a basic part of the Buddhist teaching that emotions afflict beings, giving them problems at the time and causing more problems in the future.

Awareness, Skt. jñā, Tib. shes pa: "Awareness" is always used in our translations to mean the basic knower of mind or, as Buddhist teaching itself defines it, "a general term for any registering mind", whether dualistic or non-dualistic.

Hence, it is used for both samsaric and nirvanic situations; for example, consciousness (Tib. rnam par shes pa) is a dualistic form of awareness, whereas rigpa, wisdom (Tib. ye shes), and so on are non-dualistic forms of awareness. See under rigpa.

It is noteworthy that the key term "rigpa" is often mistakenly translated as "awareness", even though it is not merely an awareness; this creates considerable confusion amongst practitioners of the higher tantras who are misled by it.

Becoming, Skt. bhāvanā, Tib. srid pa: This is another name for samsaric existence. Beings in saṃsāra have a samsaric existence but, more than that, they are constantly in a state of becoming—becoming this type of being or that type of being in this abode or that, as they are driven along without choice by the karmic process that drives samsaric existence.

Bodhichitta, Tib. byang chub sems: See under enlightenment mind.

Bodhisatva, Tib. byang chub sems dpa': A bodhisatva is a person who has engendered the bodhichitta, enlightenment mind, and, with that as a basis, has undertaken the path to the enlightenment of a truly complete buddha specifically for the welfare of other beings. Note that, despite the common appearance of "bodhisattva" in Western books on Buddhism, the Tibetan tradition has steadfastly maintained since the time of the earliest translations that the correct spelling is bodhisatva; see under satva and sattva.

Clinging, Tib. zhen pa: In Buddhism, this term refers specifically to the twofold process of dualistic mind mis-taking things that are not true, not pure, as true, pure, etcetera and then, because of seeing them as highly desirable even though they are not, attaching itself to or clinging to those things. This type of clinging acts as a kind of glue that keeps a person joined to the unsatisfactory things of cyclic existence because of mistakenly seeing them as desirable.

Complexion: Tib. mdangs: In both Mahāmudrā and Great Completion there is the general term "gdangs" meaning what is given off or emitted by something in general, for example the sound given off by a loudspeaker or what the empty factor of mind emits. The Mahāmudrā teaching does not distinguish between "gdangs" and "mdangs" but the Great Completion teaching does. In Great Completion, this term has the more refined meaning of the "complexion" or "lustre" of something. In this teaching, there is the "gdangs" output of the empty aspect of mind in general, but there is also the more subtle "mdangs" complexion or lustre which is an aspect of the output of that emptiness.

Confusion, Tib. 'khrul pa: In Buddhism, this term mostly refers to the fundamental confusion of taking things the wrong way that happens because of fundamental ignorance, although it can also have the more general meaning of having lots of thoughts and being confused about it. In the first case, it is defined like this "Confusion is the appearance to rational mind of something being present when it is not" and refers, for example, to seeing an object, such as a table, as being truly present, when in fact it is present only as mere, interdependent appearance.

Consciousness, Skt. vijñāna, Tib. rnam shes: The term means "awareness of superficies". A consciousness is a dualistic (jñā) awareness which simply registers a certain type of (vi) superfice, for example, an eye consciousness by definition registers only the superficies of visual form. A very important point is that the addition of the "vi" to the basic term (jñā) for awareness conveys the sense of a less than perfect way of being aware. This is not a wisdom awareness which knows every superfice in an utterly uncomplicated way but a limited type of awareness which is restricted to knowing one kind of superfice or another and which is part of the complicated—and highly unsatisfactory process—called (dualistic) mind. Note that this definition, which is a crucial part of understanding the role of consciousness in samsaric being, is fully conveyed by the Sanskrit and Tibetan terms but not at all by the English term.

Cross Over, Tib. la zla ba: This is a special term of Great Completion. It means to resolve in direct experience that a certain situation is that way. First you learn about the view, then you resolve or cross over into it, then you meditate on the view that has been resolved in order to fully manifest it.

Dharmadhatu, Skt. dharmadhātu, Tib. chos kyi dbyings: A *dhātu* is a place or basis from or within which something can come into being. In the case of a dharma dhātu, it is the place or space which is a basis from and in which all dharmas or phenomena, can and do come into being. If a flower bed is the place where flowers grow and are found, the dharmadhātu is the dharma or phenomena bed in which all phenomena come into being and are found. The term is used in all levels of Buddhist teaching with that general meaning but the explanation of it becomes more profound as the teaching becomes more profound. For example, in Great Completion and Mahāmudrā, it is the all-pervading sphere of luminosity-wisdom, given that luminosity is where phenomena arise and luminosity is none other than wisdom.

Dharmata, Skt. dharmatā, Tib. chos nyid: This is a general term meaning the way that something is, and can be applied to anything at all; it is similar in meaning to "actuality" *q.v.* For example, the dharmatā of water is wetness and the dharmatā of the becoming bardo is a place where beings are in a samsaric, or becoming mode, prior to entering a nature bardo. It is used frequently in Tibetan Buddhism to mean "the dharmatā of reality" but that is a specific case of the much larger meaning of the term. To read texts which use this term successfully, one has to understand that the term has a general meaning and then see how that applies in context.

Dharmín, Tib. chos can: Generally speaking a dharmin is a conceived-of phenomenon, so by implication belongs to the world of saṃsāra. It is not only a phenomenon in general, a dharma, but has become a conceptualized phenomenon because of the samsaric context. Padma Karpo defines it as "awareness possessing a phenomenon" which puts the emphasis on the samsaric awareness knowing the phenomenon.

Dhatu, Skt. dhātu, Tib. dbyings: The Sanskrit term has over twenty meanings. Many of those meanings are also present in the Tibetan equivalent. In the Vajra Vehicle teachings it is used as a replacement for the term emptiness that conveys a non-theoretical sense of the experience of emptiness. When used this way, it has the sense "expanse" because emptiness is experienced as an expanse in which all phenomena appear.

Discursive thought, Skt. vikalpa, Tib. rnam rtog: This means more than just the superficial thought that is heard as a voice in the head. It includes the entirety of conceptual process that arises due to mind contacting any object of any of the senses. The Sanskrit and Tibetan literally mean "(dualistic) thought (that arises from the mind wandering among the) various (superficies *q.v.* perceived in the doors of the senses)".

Elaboration, Tib. spro ba: This is a general name for what is given off by dualistic mind as it goes about its conceptual business. The term is pejorative in that it implies that a story has been made up, un-necessarily, about something which is actually nothing, which is empty. Elaborations, because of what they are, prevent a person from seeing emptiness directly.

Freedom from elaboration or being elaboration-free implies direct sight of emptiness. It is important to understand that these words are used in a theoretical or philosophical way in the second turning sutra teachings but are used in an experiential way in the final teachings of the third turning sutras and in the tantras of Great Completion and Mahāmudrā. In the former, being free of elaborations is a definition of what could happen according to the tenets of the Middle Way, and so on; in the latter it is a description of a state of being, one which, because it is empty of all the elaborations of dualistic being, is the actual sphere of emptiness.

Enlightenment mind, Skt. bodhichitta, Tib. byang chub sems: This is a key term of the Great Vehicle. It is the type of mind that is connected not with the lesser enlightenment of an arhat but the enlightenment of a truly complete buddha. As such, it is a mind which is connected with the aim of bringing all sentient beings to that same level of buddhahood. A person who has this mind has entered the Great Vehicle and is either a bodhisatva or a buddha.

It is important to understand that "enlightenment mind" is used to refer equally to the minds of all levels of bodhisatva on the path to buddhahood and to the mind of a buddha who has completed the path. Therefore, it is not "mind striving for enlightenment" as is so often translated, but "enlightenment mind", meaning that kind of mind which is connected with the full enlightenment of a truly complete buddha and which is present in all those who belong to the Great Vehicle. The term is used in the conventional Great Vehicle and also in the Vajra Vehicle. In the Vajra Vehicle, there are some special uses of the term where substances of the pure aspect of the subtle physical body are understood to be manifestations of enlightenment mind.

Entity, Tib. ngo bo: The entity of something is just exactly what that thing is. In English we would often simply say "thing" rather than entity. However, in Buddhism, "thing" has a very specific meaning rather than the general meaning that it has in English. It has become common to translate this term as "essence" *q.v.* However, in most cases "entity", meaning what a thing is rather than an essence of that thing, is the correct translation for this term.

Expressions, Tib. brjod pa: According to Sanskrit and Tibetan grammar following it, expressions refers to mental and verbal expressions. Thus, for example, the phrase seen in translation of "word, thought, and expression" is mistaken. The phrase is actually "expressions mental and verbal".

Fact, Skt. artha, Tib. don: "Fact" is that knowledge of an object that occurs to the surface of mind or wisdom. It is not the object but what the mind or wisdom understands as the object. Thus there are two usages of "fact": fact known to dualistic and non-dualistic minds. The higher tantras especially use "fact" to refer to the actual fact known in direct perception of actuality. Thus, there are phrases such as "in fact" which do not mean that the author is speaking truly about something but that whatever is about to be said is referring to actual fact as known to wisdom. A further complexity is that phrases such as "in fact" in those contexts are often abbreviations of "in superfact" *q.v.* This brings a further difficulty for the reader because "superfact" can be used in a general way to indicate directly perceived non-samsaric fact or can be used according to its specific definition (for which see superfact). In Buddhist tradition, problems like this are solved by having the text explained by one's teacher. That might not be possible for some readers, so uses of the word "fact" should be looked at carefully to see whether they are indicating fact in general or the factual situation of knowing reality in direct perception.

Fictional, Skt. saṃvṛtti, Tib. kun rdzob: This term is paired with the term "superfactual" *q.v.* In the past, these terms have been translated as "relative" and "absolute" respectively, but those translations are nothing like the original terms. These terms are extremely important in the Buddhist teaching so it is very important that they be corrected, but more than that, if the actual meaning of these terms is not presented, then the teaching connected with them cannot be understood.

The Sanskrit term saṃvṛtti means a deliberate invention, a fiction, a hoax. It refers to the mind of ignorance which, because of being obscured and so not seeing suchness, is not true but a fiction. The things that appear to that ignorance are therefore fictional. Nonetheless, the beings who live in this ignorance believe that the things that appear to them through the filter of ignorance are true, are real. Therefore, these beings live in fictional truth.

Fictional and superfactual: Fictional and superfactual are our greatly improved translations for "relative" and "absolute" respectively. Briefly, the original Sanskrit word for fiction means a deliberately produced *fiction* and refers to the world projected by a mind controlled by ignorance. The original word for superfact means "that *super*ior *fact* that appears on the surface of the mind of a noble one who has transcended saṃsāra" and refers to reality seen as it actually is. Relative and absolute do not convey this meaning at all and, when they are used, the meaning being presented is simply lost.

Fictional truth, Skt. saṃvṛttisatya, Tib. kun rdzob bden pa: See under fictional.

Finality obtained, Tib. gtan pa thob ba: The path of the Thorough Cut practitioner proceeds in a three step process of introduction, followed by training, followed by attaining finality. This term is sometimes translated as stability but that does not capture the full meaning. The original term means that one has gone to the point where the whole training is finalized; it has been taken to the definitive point.

Fortune, fortunate person, Tib. skal ldan: To meet with any given dharma teaching, a person must have accumulated the karmic fortune needed for such a rare opportunity, and this kind of person is then called "a fortunate one" or "fortunate person". This term is especially used in the Vajra Vehicle, whose teachings and practices are generally very hard to meet with.

Generic image, Tib. spyi don: Generic image is the technical name for one type of conceptual structure used in the operation of conceptual mind. A generic image is a concept that conceptual mind takes and uses instead of having a direct perception of the actual thing. For example, a person can have a concept of a table, a complicated operation one aspect of which is a generic image, or can have direct sight of a table, which has no operation of concept with it. Thus, for example, the process of rational, dualistic mind with its generic images can never get at something like rigpa which lies outside the reach of dualistic mind.

Grasped-grasping, Tib. gzung 'dzin: When mind is turned outwardly as it is in the normal operation of dualistic mind, it has developed two faces that appear simultaneously. Special names are given to these two faces: mind appearing in the form of the external object being referenced is called "that which is grasped" and mind appearing in the form of the consciousness that is registering it is called the "grasper" or "grasping" of it. Thus, there is the pair of terms "grasped-grasper" or "grasped-grasping". When these two terms are used, it alerts one to the fact that a Mind Only style of presentation is being discussed. This pair of terms pervades Mind Only, Middle Way, and tantric writings and is exceptionally important in all of them.

Note that one could substitute the word "apprehended" for "grasped" and "apprehender" for "grasper" or "grasping" and that would reflect one connotation of the original Sanskrit terminology. The solidified duality of grasped and grasper is nothing but an invention of dualistic thought; it has that kind of character or characteristic.

Great Vehicle, Skt. mahāyāna, Tib. theg pa chen po: The Buddha's teachings as a whole can be summed up into three vehicles where a vehicle is defined as that which can carry a person to a certain destination. The first vehicle, called the Lesser Vehicle, contains the teachings designed to get an individual moving on the spiritual path through showing the unsatisfactory state of cyclic existence and an emancipation from that. However, that path is only concerned with personal emancipation and fails to take account of all of the beings that there are in existence. There used to be eighteen schools of Lesser Vehicle in India but the only one surviving nowadays is the Theravāda of south-east Asia. The Greater Vehicle is a step up from that. The Buddha explained that it was great in comparison to the Lesser Vehicle for seven reasons. The first of those is that it is concerned with attaining the truly complete enlightenment of a truly complete buddha for the sake of every sentient being where the Lesser Vehicle is concerned only with a personal liberation that is not truly complete enlightenment and which is achieved only for the sake of that practitioner. The Great Vehicle has two divisions: a conventional form in which the path is taught in a logical, conventional way, and an unconventional form in which the path is taught in a very direct way. This latter vehicle is called the Vajra Vehicle because it takes the innermost, indestructible (vajra) fact of reality of one's own mind as the vehicle to enlightenment.

Ground, Tib. gzhi: This is the first member of the formulation of ground, path, and fruition. Ground, path, and fruition is the way that the teachings of the path of oral instruction belonging to the Vajra Vehicle are presented to students. Ground refers to the basic situation as it is.

Habituation, Tib. gom pa: Habituation is similar to but not the same as meditation (Tib. sgom pa). Where meditation is the process of creating then cultivating a certain quality which was not there before, habituation is the process of re-familiarizing yourself with a quality that is already present, even if it has become temporarily unavailable due to being covered over.

Identification, Tib. ngos bzung ba: This is the technical name for a process belonging only to dualistic mind. It is the process that uses concepts to identify this and that item of consciousness and pigeon hole it so that it can be dealt with in the general perceptual process.

Innate, Tib. gnyug ma: This is a standard term of the higher tantras used to mean the inner situation of samsaric mind, which is its in-dwelling or innate wisdom.

Intent, Tib. dgongs pa: This is the honorific form of (Tib. sems pa) meaning "to think, to comprehend", so is used to refer to an enlightened person's understanding, though the Gelugpa school is even more restrictive and uses it only for wisdom understanding of the Buddha. In some places "intent" meaning the intended meaning based on an enlightened person's understanding and in other places simply "understanding" should be understood for this term.

Intentional conduct, Tib. mos spyod: A name in the Great Vehicle for the path activities done at levels of both accumulation and connection. At this level, one is still intending to directly realize emptiness. Note that intention is the name of one of the fifty-one mental events. Thus this name implies that it is conduct still at the level of dualistic being, though it is a good mind because it intends to reach non-dualistic being. Also, by definition there is no real accomplishment until the path of seeing is reached, so there is no real accomplishment at the level of intentional conduct. Intentional conduct as non-accomplishment followed by the three paths which are levels of accomplishment is a general presentation contained in the common vehicle.

Kagyu, Tib. bka' brgyud: There are four main schools of Buddhism in Tibet—Nyingma, Kagyu, Sakya, and Gelug. Nyingma is the oldest school dating from about 800 C.E. Kagyu and Sakya both appeared in the 12th century C.E. Each of these three schools came directly from India. The Gelug school came later and did not come directly from India but came from the other three. The Nyingma school holds the tantric teachings called Great Completion (Dzogchen); the other three schools hold the tantric teachings called Mahāmudrā. Kagyu practitioners often join Nyingma practice with their Kagyu practice and Kagyu teachers often teach both, so it is common to hear about Kagyu and Nyingma together.

Knower, Tib. shes pa: "Knower" is a generic term for that which knows. There are many types of knower, with each having its own qualities and name, too. For example, *wisdom* is a non-dualistic knower, *mind* is the dualistic samsaric version of it, *consciousness* refers to the individual "registers" of samsaric mind, and so on. Sometimes a term is needed which simply says "that which knows" without further implication of what kind of knowing it might be; *knower* is one of a few terms of that sort. Knower and awareness mean the same thing in this book.

Latency, Skt. vāsanā, Tib. bag chags: The original Sanskrit has the meaning exactly of "latency". The Tibetan term translates that inexactly with "something sitting there (Tib. chags) within the environment of mind (Tib. bag)". Although it has become popular to translate this term into English with "habitual pattern", that is not its meaning. The term refers to a karmic seed that has been imprinted on the mindstream and is present there as a latency, ready and waiting to come into manifestation. Latencies manifest as appearance to the mind, both the appearances of the outer world and the appearances of the content of the inner dualistic mind.

Liveliness, Tib. rtsal: This is a key term in both Mahāmudrā and Great Completion. The term is sometimes translated as "display" or "expression" but neither is correct. The primary meaning is the ability of empty rigpa to come to life and show appearance.

Luminosity or illumination, Skt. prabhāsvara, Tib. 'od gsal ba: The core of mind has two aspects: an emptiness factor and a knowing factor. The Buddha and many Indian religious teachers used "luminosity" as a metaphor for the knowing quality of the core of mind. If in English we would say "Mind has a knowing quality", the teachers of ancient India would say, "Mind has an illuminative quality; it is like a source of light which illuminates what it knows".

This term has been translated as "clear light" but that is a mistake that comes from not understanding the etymology of the word. It does not refer to a light that has the quality of clearness (something that makes no sense, actually!) but to the illuminative property which is the nature of the empty mind.

Note also that in both Sanskrit and Tibetan Buddhist literature, this term is frequently abbreviated just to Skt. "vara" and Tib. "gsal ba" with no change of meaning. Unfortunately, this has been thought to be another word and it has then been translated with "clarity", when in fact it is just this term in abbreviation.

Mara, Skt. māra, Tib. bdud: The Sanskrit term is closely related to the word "death". Buddha spoke of four classes of extremely negative influences that have the capacity to drag a sentient being deep into saṃsāra. They are the "māras" or "kiss of death": of having a samsaric set of five skandhas; of having afflictions; of death itself; and of the son of gods, which means being seduced and taken in totally by sensuality.

Mentation, Skt. manaskāra, Tib. yid la byed pa: Mentation is the act of using the mental mind in general and is also one of the omnipresent mental events *q.v.* Its use implies the presence of dualistic mind. Non-mentating could be simply not using the dualistic mind but is usually used to imply the absence of dualistic mind, that is, the presence of wisdom.

Mind, Skt. chitta, Tib. sems: There are several terms for mind in the Buddhist tradition, each with its own, specific meaning. This term is the most general term for the samsaric type of mind. It refers to the type of mind that is produced because of fundamental ignorance of enlightened mind. Whereas the wisdom of enlightened mind lacks all complexity and knows in a non-dualistic way, this mind of un-enlightenment is a very complicated apparatus that only ever knows in a dualistic way.

Mindness, Skt. chittatā, Tib. sems nyid: Mindness is a specific term of the tantras. It is one of many terms meaning the essence of mind or the nature of mind. It conveys the sense of "what mind is at its very core". It has sometimes been translated as "mind itself" but that is a misunderstanding of the Tibetan word "nyid". The term does not mean "that thing mind" where mind refers to dualistic mind. Rather, it means the very core of dualistic mind, what mind is at root, without all of the dualistic baggage.

Mindness is a path term. It refers to exactly the same thing as "actuality" or "actuality of mind" which is a ground term but does so from the practitioner's perspective. It conveys the sense to a practitioner that he has baggage of dualistic mind that has not yet been purified but that there is a core to that mind that he can work with.

Noble one, Skt. ārya, Tib. 'phags pa: In Buddhism, a noble one is a being who has become spiritually advanced to the point that he has passed beyond cyclic existence. According to the

Buddha, the beings in cyclic existence were ordinary beings, spiritual commoners, and the beings who had passed beyond it were special, the nobility.

Non-regressing, Tib. phyir mi ldogs pa: This is a standard term used to describe the ultimate teachings on emptiness of the third turning of the wheel of dharma, called Other Emptiness. When a person has heard and comprehended these teachings, he immediately understands that all other teachings of the second and third turnings of the wheel are not ultimate and assumes the position that he will never turn back from these teachings and regress to taking one of the lesser views as ultimate. The "non-regressing path" mentioned in this book is a reference to the path of wisdom taught both in the third turning of the wheel of dharma and the tantras.

Overstatement, Tib. skur 'debs pa: In Buddhism, this term is used in two ways. Firstly, it is used in general to mean misunderstanding from the perspective that one has added more to one's understanding of something than needs to be there. Secondly, it is used specifically to indicate that dualistic mind always overstates or exaggerates whatever object it is examining. Dualistic mind always adds the ideas of solidity, permanence, singularity, and so on to everything it references via the concepts that it uses. Severing of exaggeration either means removal of these un-necessary mis-understandings when trying to properly comprehend something or removal of the dualistic process altogether when trying to get to the non-dualistic reality of a phenomenon.

Prajna, Skt. prajñā, Tib. shes rab: The Sanskrit term, literally meaning "best type of mind" is defined as that which makes correct distinctions between this and that and hence which arrives at correct understanding. It has been translated as "wisdom" but that is not correct because it is, generally speaking, a mental event belonging to dualistic mind where "wisdom" is used to refer to the non-dualistic knower of a buddha. Moreover, the main feature of prajñā is its ability to distinguish correctly between one thing and another and hence to arrive at a correct understanding.

Preserve, Tib. skyong ba: This term is important in both Mahāmudrā and Great Completion. In general, it means to defend, protect, nurture, maintain. In the higher tantras it means to keep something just as it is, to nurture that something so that it stays and is not lost. Also, in the higher tantras, it is often used in reference to preserving the state where the state is some particular state of being. Because of this, the phrase "preserve the state" is an important instruction in the higher tantras.

Rational mind, Tib. blo: Rational mind is one of several terms for mind in Buddhist terminology. It specifically refers to a mind that judges this against that. With rare exception it is used to refer to samsaric mind, given that samsaric mind only works in the dualistic mode of comparing this versus that. Because of this, the term is mostly used in a pejorative sense to point out samsaric mind as opposed to an enlightened type of mind.

Realization, Tib. rtogs pa: Realization has a very specific meaning: it refers to correct knowledge that has been gained in such a way that the knowledge does not abate. There are two important points here. Firstly, realization is not absolute. It refers to the removal of obscurations, one at a time. Each time that a practitioner removes an obscuration, he gains a realization because of it. Therefore, there are as many levels of realization as there are obscurations. Maitreya, in the *Ornament of Manifest Realizations,* shows how the removal of the various obscurations that go with each of the three realms of samsaric existence produces realization.

Reference and Referencing, Tib. dmigs pa: Referencing is the name for the process in which dualistic mind references an actual object by using a conceptual label instead of the actual object. Whatever is referenced is then called a reference. Note that these terms imply the presence of dualistic mind and their opposites, non-referencing and being without reference imply the presence of non-dualistic wisdom.

Rigpa, Tib. rig pa: This is the singularly most important term in the whole of Great Completion and Mahāmudrā. In particular, it is the key word of all words in the Great Completion system of the Thorough Cut. Rigpa literally means to know in the sense of "I see!" It is used at all levels of meaning from the coarsest everyday sense of knowing something to the deepest sense of knowing something as presented in the Great Completion teachings of Thorough Cut. The system of Thorough Cut uses this term in a very special sense, though it still retains its basic meaning of "to know". To translate it as "awareness", which is common practice today, is a poor practice; there are many kinds of awareness but there is only one rigpa and besides, rigpa is substantially more than just awareness. Since this is such an important term and since it lacks an equivalent in English, I choose not to translate it.

Samsara, Skt. saṃsāra, Tib. 'khor ba: This is the most general name for the type of existence in which sentient beings live. It refers to the fact that they continue on from one existence to another, always within the enclosure of births that are produced by ignorance and experienced as unsatisfactory. The original Sanskrit means to be constantly going about, here and there. The Tibetan term literally means "cycling", because of which it is frequently translated into English with "cyclic existence" though that is not quite the meaning of the term.

Satva and sattva: According to the Tibetan tradition established at the time of the great translation work done at Samye under the watch of Padmasambhava not to mention one hundred and sixty-three of the greatest Buddhist scholars of Sanskrit-speaking India, there is a difference of meaning between the Sanskrit terms "satva" and "sattva", with satva meaning "an heroic kind of being" and "sattva" meaning simply "a being". According to the Tibetan tradition established under the advice of the Indian scholars mentioned above, satva is correct for the words Vajrasatva and bodhisatva, whereas sattva is correct for the words samayasattva, samādhisattva, and jñānasattva, and is also used alone to refer to any or all of these three satvas.

Shine forth, shining forth, Tib. shar ba: This term means "to dawn" or "to come forth into visibility" either in the outer physical world or in the inner world of mind.

It is heavily used in texts on meditation to indicate the process of something coming forth into mind. There are other terms with this specific meaning but most of them also imply the process of dawning within a samsaric mind. "Shine forth" is special because it does not have that restricted meaning; it refers to the process of something dawning in any type of mind, un-enlightened and enlightened. It is an important term for the higher tantras of Mahāmudrā and Great Completion texts where there is a great need to refer to the simple fact of something dawning in mind especially in enlightened mind but also in un-enlightened mind.

State, Tib. ngang: A state is a certain, ongoing situation. In Buddhist meditation in general, there are various states that a practitioner has to enter and remain in as part of developing the meditation.

Superfactual, Skt. paramārtha, Tib. don dam: This term is paired with the term "fictional" *q.v.* In the past, the terms have been translated as "relative" and "absolute" respectively, but those translations are nothing like the original terms. These terms are extremely important in the Buddhist teaching so it is very important that their translations be corrected but, more than that, if the actual meaning of these terms is not presented, the teaching connected with them cannot be understood.

The Sanskrit term literally means "the fact for that which is above all others, special, superior" and refers to the wisdom mind possessed by those who have developed themselves spiritually to the point of having transcended saṃsāra. That wisdom is *superior* to an ordinary, un-developed person's consciousness and the *facts* that appear on its surface are superior compared to the facts that appear on the ordinary person's consciousness. Therefore, it is superfact or the holy fact, more literally. What this wisdom knows is true for the beings who have it, therefore what the wisdom sees is superfactual truth.

Superfactual truth, Skt. paramārthasatya, Tib. don dam bden pa: See under superfactual.

The authentic, Tib. yang dag: A name for reality, that which is real. For example "the view of the authentic" means "the view of reality" not a correct view.

Unsatisfactoriness, Skt. duḥkha, Tib. sdug bngal: This term is usually translated into English with "suffering" but there are many problems with that. When the Buddha talked about the nature of samsaric existence, he said that it was unsatisfactory. He used the term "duḥkha", which includes actual suffering but means much more than that. Duḥkha is one of a pair of terms, the other being "sukha", which is usually translated as, but does not only mean, bliss. The real meaning of duḥkha is "everything on the side of bad"—not good, uncomfortable, unpleasant, not nice, and so on. Thus, it means "unsatisfactory in every possible way". The real meaning of its opposite, sukha, is "everything on the side of good"—not bad, comfortable, pleasant, nice, and so on. Therefore, that he is completely liberated from the sufferings actually means that he has completely liberated himself from the unsatisfactoriness of samsara, which includes all types of suffering and happiness, too.

Wisdom, Skt. jñāna, Tib. ye shes: This is a fruition term that refers to the kind of mind—the kind of knower—possessed by a buddha. Sentient beings do have this kind of knower but it is covered over by a very complex apparatus for knowing, that is, dualistic mind. If they practise the path to buddhahood, they will leave behind their obscuration and return to having this kind of knower.

The Sanskrit term has the sense of knowing in the most simple and immediate way. This sort of knowing is present at the core of every being's mind. Therefore, the Tibetans called it "the particular type of awareness which is there primordially". Because of the Tibetan wording it has often been called "primordial wisdom" in English translations, but that goes too far; it is just "wisdom" in the sense of the most fundamental knowing possible.

Wisdom does not operate in the same way as samsaric mind; it comes about in and of itself without depending on cause and effect. Therefore it is frequently referred to as "self-arising wisdom" *q.v.*

ABOUT THE AUTHOR, PADMA KARPO TRANSLATIONS, AND THEIR SUPPORTS FOR STUDY

I have been encouraged over the years by all of my teachers to pass on the knowledge I have accumulated in a lifetime dedicated to study and practice, primarily in the Tibetan tradition of Buddhism. On the one hand, they have encouraged me to teach. On the other, they are concerned that, while many general books on Buddhism have been and are being published, there are few books that present the actual texts of the tradition. Therefore they, together with a number of major figures in the Buddhist book publishing world, have also encouraged me to translate and publish high quality translations of individual texts of the tradition.

My teachers always remark with great appreciation on the extraordinary amount of teaching that I have heard in this life. It allows for highly informed, accurate translations of a sort not usually seen. Briefly, I spent the 1970's studying, practising, then teaching the Gelugpa system at Chenrezig Institute, Australia, where I was a founding member and also the first Australian to be ordained as a monk in the Tibetan Buddhist tradition. In 1980, I moved to the United States to study at the feet of the Vidyadhara Chogyam Trungpa Rinpoche. I stayed in his Vajradhatu community, now called Shambhala, where I studied and practised all the Karma Kagyu, Nyingma, and Shambhala teachings being presented there and was a senior member of the Nalanda Translation Committee. After the vidyadhara's nirvana, I moved in 1992 to Nepal, where I have been continuously involved with the study, practise, translation, and teaching of the Kagyu system and especially of the Nyingma system of Great Completion. In recent years, I have spent extended times in Tibet with the greatest living Tibetan masters of Great Completion, receiving very pure transmissions of the ultimate levels of this teaching directly in Tibetan and practising them there in retreat. In that way, I have studied and practised extensively not in one Tibetan tradition as is usually done, but in three of the four Tibetan traditions—Gelug, Kagyu, and Nyingma—and also in the Theravada tradition, too.

With that as a basis, I have taken a comprehensive and long term approach to the work of translation. For any language, one first must have the lettering needed to write the language. Therefore, as a member of the Nalanda Translation Committee, I spent some years in the 1980's making Tibetan word-processing software and high-quality Tibetan fonts. After that, reliable lexical works are needed. Therefore, during the 1990's I spent some years writing the *Illuminator Tibetan-English Dictionary* and a set of treatises on Tibetan grammar, preparing a variety of key Tibetan reference works needed for the study and translation of Tibetan Buddhist texts, and giving our Tibetan software the tools needed to translate and research Tibetan texts. During this time, I also translated full-time for various Tibetan gurus and ran the Drukpa Kagyu

Heritage Project—at the time the largest project in Asia for the preservation of Tibetan Buddhist texts. With the dictionaries, grammar texts, and specialized software in place, and a wealth of knowledge, I turned my attention in the year 2000 to the translation and publication of important texts of Tibetan Buddhist literature.

Padma Karpo Translation Committee (PKTC) was set up to provide a home for the translation and publication work. The committee focusses on producing books containing the best of Tibetan literature, and, especially, books that meet the needs of practitioners. At the time of writing, PKTC has published a wide range of books that, collectively, make a complete program of study for those practising Tibetan Buddhism, and especially for those interested in the higher tantras. All in all, you will find many books both free and for sale on the PKTC web-site. Most are available both as paper editions and e-books.

It would take up too much space here to present an extensive guide to our books and how they can be used as the basis for a study program. However, a guide of that sort is available on the PKTC web-site, whose address is on the copyright page of this book and we recommend that you read it to see how this book fits into the overall scheme of PKTC publications.

We make a point of including, where possible, the relevant Tibetan texts in Tibetan script in our books. We also make them available in electronic editions that can be downloaded free from our web-site, as discussed below. The Tibetan text for this book is included at the back of the book.

Electronic Resources

PKTC has developed a complete range of electronic tools to facilitate the study and translation of Tibetan texts. For many years now, this software has been a prime resource for Tibetan Buddhist centres throughout the world, including in Tibet itself. It is available through the PKTC web-site.

The wordprocessor TibetDoc has the only complete set of tools for creating, correcting, and formatting Tibetan text according to the norms of the Tibetan language. It can also be used to make texts with mixed Tibetan and English or other languages. Extremely high quality Tibetan fonts, based on the forms of Tibetan calligraphy learned from old masters from pre-Communist Chinese Tibet, are also available. Because of their excellence, these typefaces have achieved a legendary status amongst Tibetans.

TibetDoc is used to prepare electronic editions of Tibetan texts in the PKTC text input office in Asia. Tibetan texts are often corrupt so the input texts are carefully corrected prior to distribution. After that, they are made available through the PKTC web-site. These electronic texts are not careless productions like so many of the Tibetan texts found on the web, but are highly reliable editions useful to non-scholars and scholars alike. Some of the larger collections of these texts are for purchase, but most are available for free download.

The electronic texts can be read, searched, and even made into an electronic library using either TibetDoc or our other software, TibetD Reader. Like TibetDoc, TibetD Reader is advanced software with many capabilities made specifically to meet the needs of reading and researching Tibetan texts. PKTC software is for purchase but we make a free version of TibetD Reader available for free download on the PKTC web-site.

A key feature of TibetDoc and Tibet Reader is that Tibetan terms in texts can be looked up on the spot using PKTC's electronic dictionaries. PKTC also has several electronic dictionaries—some Tibetan-Tibetan and some Tibetan-English—and a number of other reference works. The *Illuminator Tibetan-English Dictionary* is renowned for its completeness and accuracy.

This combination of software, texts, reference works, and dictionaries that work together seamlessly has become famous over the years. It has been the basis of many, large publishing projects within the Tibetan Buddhist community around the world for over thirty years and is popular amongst all those needing to work with Tibetan language or deepen their understanding of Buddhism through Tibetan texts.

TIBETAN TEXT

༄༅། །ཐེག་ཆེན་བླ་བྲིད་བདེན་གཉིས་རབ་ཏུ་གསལ་བ་ཞེས་བྱ་བ་བཞུགས་སོ།།

༄༅། །ཁར་འདོད་རྣམས་ཀྱིས་རྟོགས་པར་བྱ་བའི་ཆོས་དང་། རྣམས་སུ་སྣང་བའི་ཆོས་གཉིས། དང་པོ་ལའང་ཤེས་བྱ་སྟོའི་གནས་ལུགས་དང་། ཤེས་པ་རང་གི་གནས་ལུགས་གཉིས། དང་པོ་ལའང་ཀུན་རྫོབ་དང་དོན་དམ་གཉིས་ལས། དང་པོ་ནི། སྒྱུར་དགུལ་བ་མནར་མེད་པ་ནས་ས་བཅུའི་རྟེན་ཐོབ་མན་ཆད་ཀྱི་སྣང་བ་ཐམས་ཅད་ཀུན་རྫོབ་ཡིན། དེ་ལའང་ལོག་པའི་ཀུན་རྫོབ་དང་ཡང་དག་གཉིས་ལས། ལས་དང་པོ་ལ་མན་ཆད་ལ་སྣང་ཚད་ལོག་པའི་ཀུན་རྫོབ། མོས་པ་སྤྱོད་པ་རྣམས་ལ་རྟོགས་པའི་རྟེས་ཟིན་པའི་དུས་ན་སྣང་བ་ཐམས་ཅད་ཡང་དག་ཀུན་རྫོབ། མ་ཟིན་དུས་ན་ལོག་རྟོག་ཡིན། ས་ཐོབ་ནས་ཡིད་ལ་སྣང་ཚད་ཡང་དག་ཀུན་རྟོབ་ཡིན། སྣང་ཙམ་མ་འགགས་པས་ཀུན་རྟོབ་ཡིན་ལ་དེ་ཉིད་སྟོན་པར་མངོན་སུམ་ཀྱིས་གཟིགས་པས་སོ། ། ས་དང་པོ་ནས་ས་བཅུའི་བར་གྱི་སྣང་བ་དེ་དག་ཀྱང་སྤྱིར་དངོས་འཛིན་ལ་ཡུན

རིན་པོར་གོམས་པའི་བག་ཆགས་མ་སྨྱུང་བས་བསྐྱེད་པ་སྟེ་སྔ་རྩིའི་སྡོད་ཀྱི་རི་དང་འདྲ། བག་ཆགས་ཙུད་ནས་སྨྱངས་པའི་གངས་རྒྱས་ལ་སྨྱུང་བ་གང་ཡང་མེད། དེ་དོན་དམ་པར་སྟོབས་བྲལ་འབའ་ཞིག་ཏུ་གནས་སོ། །ཁ་མ་ལ་གྱི་སྡོད་བཏུད་ལ་དངོས་པོར་ཞེན་པ་ནི་ལོག་རྟོག་ཡིན། དེའི་གཉེན་པོར་དག་པའི་ལྷ་དང་གཞལ་ཡས་ཁང་སྒྱུ་མ་ལྟ་བུར་བསྒྱུར་ནས་སྣོགས་པ་སོགས་ཡང་དག་ཀུན་རྫོབ་ཡིན། གཉིས་པ་དོན་དམ་པའི་དོ་བོའི་ཆོས་ཀྱི་དབྱིངས་སྟོགས་པ་དང་བྲལ་བ་ཡིན། དེའི་དོ་བོ་ལ་འབྱེར་མེད་ཀྱང་། དེ་ཉིད་མདོན་དུ་གྱུར་མ་གྱུར་གྱི་སྒོག་པ་ནས་དབྱེ་ན། རང་བཞིན་གཤིས་ཀྱི་དང་། དེ་ཉིད་རྟོགས་པ་མདོན་གྱུར་ཀྱིས་འམ། ཡང་ན་ཐོས་བསམ་གྱི་སྒོ་འདོགས་ཆོད་པའི་དང་། རྣལ་འབྱོར་པས་ཉམས་སུ་སྨྱོང་བ་འམ། སོ་སྐྱེས་དོན་སྤྱི་རྟེས་དཔག་གི་དང་། འཕགས་པས་རང་རིག་མདོན་གསུམ་གྱི་དོན་དམ་པ་སྟེ། དེ་ཡང་རྣམ་གྲངས་ཀྱི་དང་། རྣམ་གྲངས་མ་ཡིན་པའི་དོན་དམ་ཞེས་གསུངས་སོ། །བདེན་པ་གཉིས་པོ་དེ་ལ་སྨྱུང་ལུགས་གསུམ་ཡོད་དེ། སྨྱུང་བ་རང་རྒྱུད་པར་སྨྱུང་ཞིང་ཞེན་པ་དང་བཅས་པ་ནི་སོ་སོའི་སྐྱེ་བོའི་ས་སྟེ། དེ་ལ་ལོག་པའི་ཀུན་རྟོག་ཟེར། སྨྱུང་བ་རྟུན་པར་རྟོགས་ཤིང་ཞེན་པ་མེད་པ་འཕགས་པའི་ས་དེ་ལ་ཡང་དག་པའི་ཀུན་རྟོག་ཅེས་བྱ། སྨྱུང་བ་དང་མི་སྨྱུང་བ་གང་ཡང་མེད་ཅིང་ཞེན་མི་ཞེན་གྱི་ཆེས་གདབ་དང་བྲལ་བ་སངས་རྒྱས་ཀྱི་ས་སྟེ། དེ་ག་ལ་དོན་དམ་ཞེས་བྱའོ། །དེ་ཡང་དང་པོ་ལ་སྨྱུང་ཞེན་གཉིས་ཀ་ཡོད། བར་མ་ལ་སྨྱུང་ཙམ་ལས་ཞེན་པ་མེད། ཕྱི་མ་ལ་སྨྱུང་ཞེན་གཉིས་ཀ་མེད་དོ། །དེ་གསུམ་ཡང་ལོག་པའི་ཤེས་པ་དང་། ཀུན་རྟོག་ཤེས་པའི་ཤེས་པ་དང་། དོན་དམ་ཤེས་པའི་ཤེས་པའོ། །སོ་སོའི་སྐྱེ་བོའི་ཀུན་རྟོག་ཤེས་པའི་ཤེས་རབ་ན་བརྟག་དཔྱད་ལ་རགས་ལས་སོ། །འཕགས་པས་ནི་མདོན་སུམ་པའོ། །དོན་དམ་པའི

ཆོས་ཀྱི་དབྱིངས་ལ་ཤེས་མི་ཤེས་ཀྱི་ཐ་སྙད་མེད་ཀྱང་། དེ་ཉིད་ཁོང་དུ་ཆུད་པ་ལ་ཤེས་པའམ་རྟོགས་པ་སོགས་སུ་བཏགས་སོ། །མཐར་ཐུག་བདེན་གཉིས་དབྱེར་མེད་དུ་རྟོགས་པར་བྱ་བ་ནི། ཀུན་རྫོབ་ཅེས་ཡོད་ཡོད་པོ་དང་། དོན་དམ་ཞེས་མེད་མེད་པོར་བཏགས་པ་དབུ་མའི་ལྟ་བར་མི་འགྱུར་ཏེ། ཡང་དག་ཀུན་རྫོབ་རྣལ་མ་གཅིག་རྟོགས་པའི་དུས་རང་ནས་ཡོད་མེད་དགག་ཆད་ཀྱི་མཐའ་ཐམས་ཅད་དང་བྲལ་བ་བདེན་པ་གཉིས་དབྱེར་མེད་དུ་འདྲེས་པ་ཡིན་ཏེ། ཡུམ་ལས། ཀུན་རྫོབ་ཀྱི་དེ་ཁོ་ན་ཉིད་གང་ཡིན་པ་དེ་ཉིད་དོན་དམ་པའི་དེ་ཁོ་ན་ཉིད་དོ། །ཞེས་སོ། །བདེན་པ་གཉིས་སུ་དབྱེ་བའང་། རེ་ཞིག་ཤེས་རོ་གཉིས་ལ་སྣོས་ནས་རྟོགས་སླ་བའི་ཆེད་དུ་བཏགས་པ་ཙམ་སྟེ། དེ་ཡང་འཁྲུལ་པའི་ཤེས་རོ་ལ་དངོས་པོ་སྣ་ཚོགས་སུ་སྣང་བ་ཀུན་རྫོབ་ཏུ་བཏགས། འཁྲུལ་པ་ཟད་པའི་ཤེས་རོ་ལ་རྟུལ་ཚམ་ཡང་མེད་ཅིང་མེད་པས་རང་ཡང་མི་དམིགས་པས་དོན་དམ་ཞེས་བཏགས་པ་ཡིན་ཏེ། གང་ཚེ་དངོས་དང་དངོས་མེད་དག ། བློ་ཡི་མདུན་ན་མི་གནས་པ། ། དེ་ཚེ་རྣམ་པ་གཞན་མེད་པས། །དམིགས་པ་མེད་པར་རབ་ཏུ་ཞི། །ཞེས་སོ། །དོན་ལ་ཤེས་བྱ་མི་གཞིས་མཐར་ཐུག་ཆོས་ཀྱི་དབྱིངས་སྟོངས་ཐལ་ཆེན་པོ་ལ་བདེན་པ་གཉིས་སུ་དབྱེ་བའི་གདགས་གཞི་མ་གྲུབ་པས་དབྱེ་རུ་མེད། མཐར་ཕྱིན་པའི་སངས་རྒྱས་ཀྱི་དགོངས་པ་ལའང་བདེན་པ་གཉིས་སུ་དབྱེ་རྒྱུ་མེད། ད་ལྟར་གྱི་འཁྲུལ་སྣང་འདི་ལ་ཡང་བདེན་པ་གཉིས་ཐ་དད་དུ་མ་གྲུབ་སྟེ། སྣང་སྟོང་དབྱེར་མེད་རིག་སྟོང་དབྱེར་མེད་དུ་གནས་ཤིང་། དེ་ལྟར་རྟོགས་པའམ་ཁོང་དུ་ཆུད་པ་དེ་ཉིད་སངས་རྒྱས་ཀྱི་དགོངས་པ་ཆོས་ཉིད་གཉིས་སུ་མེད་པའི་ཡེ་ཤེས་ཡིན་ཏེ། བདེན་གཉིས་སོ་སོའི་ཚ་ཡང་དག་པར་ཤེས་ཤིང་དེ་གཉིས་དབྱེར་མེད་དུ་འདྲེས་པར་འགྱུར་པ་ལ་བྱང་འཇུག་གཉིས་སུ་མེད་པའི་ཡེ་ཤེས་དང་མི་གནས་པའི་མྱ་ངན་

ལས་འདས་པ་སོགས་སུ་བཏགས་སོ། །དེ་ལྟར་ཡུལ་ཤེས་བྱ་སྟྱིའི་གནས་ལུགས་རྟོགས་ཀྱང་། ཡུལ་ཅན་ཤེས་པ་རང་གི་གནས་ལུགས་མ་རྟོགས་ན། ཆོས་ཐམས་ཅད་ཤེས་བྱའི་ཡུལ་དུ་ཡུལ་ནས་ཉིན་མོངས་པའི་གཉེན་པོར་མི་འགྲོ་སྟེ་རྟོགས་པ་དེ་ཉིད་ལས་ང་རྒྱལ་དང་རློམ་སེམས་སྐྱེ་ཞིང་། གང་ཟག་གི་བདག་རགས་སུ་འགྲོ་བས། ཤེས་བྱ་ཤེས་མཁན་གྱི་བློ་འདས་སེམས་སམ། ཡིད་དམ་རྣམ་ཤེས་ཁོ་རང་གི་གནས་ལུགས་རྟོགས་དགོས། དེ་ལ་གཉིས་ཏེ། རེ་ཞིག་བདེན་པ་གཉིས་སུ་རྟོགས་པར་བྱ་བ་དང་། མཐར་ཐུག་བདེན་པ་དབྱེར་མེད་དུ་རྟོགས་པར་བྱ་བའོ། །དང་པོ་ནི། ཤེས་བྱ་སྟྱིའི་གནས་ལུགས་ཀུན་རྫོབ་སྒྱུ་ལ་རང་བཞིན་མེད་པར་སྒྱུ་མ་ལྟ་བུར་རྟོགས། དོན་དམ་པར་ཡོད་མེད་ཅིར་ཡང་མ་གྲུབ་པ་རྣམ་མཁའ་ལྟ་བུར་རྟོགས། མཐར་ཐུག་བདེན་པ་གཉིས་དབྱེར་མེད་ཆོས་ཀྱི་དབྱིངས་སུ་མཐའི་སྤྲོས་པ་ཐམས་ཅད་བྲལ་བའི་དབུ་མ་ཆེན་པོར་རྟོགས་པའི་བློ་འདས་ཤེས་པ་དེ་ཉིད་ཀུན་རྫོབ་ཡིན་ཏེ། ཞི་བ་ལྷས། དེ་ན་དམ་བློ་ཡི་སྤྱོད་ཡུལ་མིན། །བློའི་ཀུན་རྫོབ་ཡིན་པར་འདོད། །ཅེས་སོ། །དེ་ལྟར་རྟོགས་པའི་བློ་གང་ཡོད་པ་དེ་ལ་ང་རྒྱལ་དང་རློམ་སེམས་ཡོད་ཅིང་། ང་རྒྱལ་དང་རློམ་སེམས་ནི་བདུད་ཀྱི་ལས་ཡིན་པས་དེ་ཉིད་ལོག་ཤེས་འགྲོ་སྟེ། སངས་རྒྱས་ཀྱི་ཡུལ་བསམ་གྱིས་མི་ཁྱབ་པ་བསྟན་པའི་མདོ་ལས། ཐུབ་པ་ཞེས་བྱ་བ་ནི་གཡོ་བ་ཉིད་དོ། །མཛིན་པར་རྟོགས་པ་ཞེས་བྱ་བ་ནི་རློམ་སེམས་པ་ཉིད་དོ། །གཡོ་བ་དང་རློམ་སེམས་གང་ཡིན་པ་དེ་ནི་བདུད་ཀྱི་ལས་སོ། །སྤྱུག་པའི་ང་རྒྱལ་ཅན་དགའ་ནི་བདག་གིས་ཐོབ་བོ། །བདག་གིས་མངོན་པར་རྟོགས་སོ་ཞེས་རྣམ་པར་རྟོག་པར་འགྱུར་རོ། །ཞེས་གསུངས་སོ། །རྟོགས་པའི་བློ་ནི་ཀུན་རྫོབ་ཀྱི་རང་བཞིན་དོན་དམ་པ་ཡིན་ཏེ། རྟོགས་པའི་བློ་འདས། སེམས་སམ་ཤེས་པ་དེ་ཉིད་རང་ལ་བལྟས་པས་དངོས་

པོ་ཅེར་ཡང་མ་གྲུབ་སྟེ། ཡེ་ནས་ཡོད་མེད་ཀྱིས་སྟོང་། སྐྱེ་འགགས་ཀྱིས་སྟོང་། འགྲོ་འོང་གིས་སྟོང་། རྟག་ཆད་ཀྱིས་སྟོང་། དུས་གསུམ་གྱིས་སྟོང་པས་ན་ཆོས་ཉིད་དོན་དམ་པ་ཞེས་བྱུ་སྟེ། འོད་སྲུང་གིས་ཞུས་པའི་མདོ་ལས། སེམས་ནི་ནང་ནའང་མེད་དེ་ཕྱི་རོལ་ནའང་མེད། །གཉིས་ཀ་མེད་པར་མི་དམིགས་སོ། །ཞེས་དང་། བྱམས་ཞུས་ལས། སེམས་ནི་དབྱིབས་མེད་པ། ཁ་དོག་མེད་པ། གནས་མེད་པ། ནམ་མཁའ་ལྟ་བུའོ། །ཞེས་གསུངས་སོ། །སེམས་ཀྱི་གནས་ལུགས་མཚར་ཕྱགས་བདེན་པ་གཉིས་དབྱེར་མེད་དུ་གནས་ཏེ། སེམས་ཉིད་གཅིག་ལ་བདེན་པ་གཉིས་སུ་བདགས་པ་དེ་ཡང་རེ་ཞིག་མིང་ཚམ་བརྡ་ཚམ། བརྡགས་པ་ཚམ་དུ་ཟད་དོ། །གཞི་ཆོས་ཀྱི་དབྱིངས་ལ་སེམས་མེད་པས་བདེན་པ་གཉིས་ཀྱི་གདགས་གཞི་མ་གྲུབ། འདས་བུ་སངས་རྒྱས་ཀྱི་དགོངས་པ་ལ་སེམས་མེད་པས་བདེན་པ་གཉིས་གདགས་སུ་མེད། འཁྲུལ་པའི་སེམས་ཅན་གྱི་སེམས་ཉིད་གསལ་སྟོང་འདི་ལ་ཡང་དོས་བཟུང་མེད་དེ། རིག་པ་གསལ་སྟོང་དུ་གནས་པས་བདེན་པ་གཉིས་དབྱེར་མེད་དུ་རྟོགས་པར་བྱའོ། །བདེན་གཉིས་དབྱེར་མེད་ཀྱི་དོན་དེ་ཡང་བདེན་པ་གཉིས་ཀྱི་མཚན་ཉིད་ཞེས་པ་ལ་བརྟེན་ནས་རྟོགས་པའི་དགོས་པ་ཡོད་པས་གཉིས་སུ་དབྱེ་བའོ། །དེ་ལྟར་ཞེས་བྱའི་གནས་ལུགས་སྟོབས་ཐབ་དང་གནས་ལུགས་སྟོབས་ཐབ་གཉིས་དབྱེར་མེད་རོ་གཅིག་ཏུ་འཇེས་ཏེ་དེའི་ཚོས་དང་གང་ཟག་གིས་སྟོང་ཚམ་ན་ཕྱི་ནང་གི་ཆོས་ཐམས་ཅད་ཡོད་མེད་རྟག་ཆད་ཀྱི་སྤྲོས་པ་ཐམས་ཅད་དང་བྲལ་ནས་འདུས་མ་བྱས་ཀྱི་ནམ་མཁའ་ལྟ་བུ་མཐོང་བུ་མཐོང་བྱེད་མེད། རྟོགས་བྱ་རྟོགས་བྱེད་མེད་པའི་ཆུལ་གྱིས་རྟོགས་ཤིང་མཐོང་བ་དེ་ཕྱིན་ཅི་མ་ལོག་པའི་རྟོགས་པ་ཡིན་ནོ། །དའི་རྣམས་སུ་བྱངས་པའི་ཆོས་བསྟན་པ་ལ་གཉིས་ལས། དབང་པོ་རྣོན་པོས་ཅིག

ཆར་དུ་ཉམས་སུ་བླང་བ་ནི། སྟོན་ཚོགས་གཉིས་བསགས་པའི་རྒྱུ་ཅན། ཟབ་མོའི་ལམ་འཕོ་དང་སྐལ་པར་ལྡན་པའི་ལམ་ཅན་དགའ་ལ་བརྟེན་པ་གཉིས་ཀྱི་གདམས་པ་བསྟན་པ་ཚམ་གྱིས་རྟོགས་པ་འཆར་བས། རྟོགས་པའི་འདང་དུ་ཉིད་ལ་བསྐྱངས་པ་ཆོག་གོ །དེ་ཡང་མཉམ་བཞག་ལ་ཤེས་པ་དང་ཤེས་བྱ་གཉིས་ཀས་སྟོང་ཞིང་བདག་མེད་པ། བདེན་པ་གཉིས་ཀྱི་སྟོས་པ་དང་བྲལ་བ་ནམ་མཁའ་ལྟ་བུའི་དང་ལ་སློབ། དེ་ལྟར་སློམས་པའི་དུས་ན་རྣམ་རྟོག་དན་པ་གཅིག་པར་བསལ་རྒྱུ་མེད། སེམས་བཟང་པོ་གཅིག་ལ་བློ་གཏད་དུ་མེད་དེ། བྱམས་མགོན་གྱིས། འདི་ལ་བསལ་བྱ་ཅི་ཡང་མེད། །བཞག་པར་བྱ་བ་ཅུང་ཟད་མེད། །ཡང་དག་ཉིད་ལ་ཡང་དག་བལྟ། །ཡང་དག་མཐོང་ན་རྣམ་པར་གྲོལ། །ཞེས་གསུངས་སོ། །རྗེས་ལ་རྗེ་ལྟར་སྣང་བ་ཐམས་ཅད་སྣང་ལ་རང་བཞིན་མེད་པ། བདེན་གཉིས་ཟུང་འཇུག་སྒྱུ་ལམ་ལྟ་བུའི་དང་དུ་བསྐྱངས། དེ་མ་རྟོགས་པའི་སེམས་ཅན་སྐྱི་ལམ་སྒྱུ་མ་ལྟ་བུ་རྣམས་ལ་བྱམས་པ་དང་སྙིང་རྗེ་བྱང་ཆུབ་ཀྱི་སེམས་སྒྱུ་མ་ཚམ་གྱིས་སེམས་ཅན་གྱི་དོན་དུ་ཚོགས་གཉིས་སྒྱུ་མ་ཚམ་གསོག་ཅིང་། སེམས་ཅན་གྱི་དོན་དུ་སྟོན་ལམ་རྒྱ་ཆེན་པོ་གདབ་པར་བྱའོ། །དབང་དུལ་རྣམས་ཀྱིས་ནི་བློ་ལྡོག་བཞི་པོ་ནས་བཟུང་སྟེ་རིམ་གྱིས་གོམས་པར་བྱ་དགོས་ཏེ། དེ་ལྟར་མ་བྱས་ན་ཟབ་མོའི་རྟོགས་པ་དོན་སྙིང་རྣམ་པ་ཚམ་ལས་མི་སྐྱེའོ། །ཇི་ལྟར་དན་སྣང་ཐམས་ཅད་ཀུན་རྗོབ་ཡིན། །དེ་ཡི་རང་བཞིན་རྟོགས་པ་དོན་དམ་མོ། །དེ་ལྟར་རྟོགས་པའི་བློའི་ཀུན་རྗོབ་ལ། །བློ་ལ་རང་བཞིན་མེད་པ་དོན་དམ་མོ། །བདེན་གཉིས་བརྗོད་པའི་སྒྲ་དེ་ཀུན་རྗོབ་ལ། །སྒྲ་ལ་རང་བཞིན་མེད་པ་དོན་དམ་མོ། །དེ་དག་གཉིས་མེད་བདེན་གཉིས་ཟུང་འཇུག་སྟེ། །ཤེས་བྱའི་གཤིས་དང་སངས་རྒྱས་དགོངས་པ་ལ། །བདེན་གཉིས་ཟུང་འཇུག་དག་ཀྱང་མི་དམིགས་པས།

ཆོས་ཀྱི་དབྱིངས་ཉིད་སློས་དང་བྲལ་ཞེས་བྱ། །དེ་ལ་གང་ཟག་ཆོས་ཀྱི་བདག་མ་གྲུབ། །དེ་ལྟར་རྟོགས་པ་གང་དེ་ལྟ་བ་ཡིན། །དེ་ཡི་རང་ལ་གནས་པ་སྒོམ་པ་ཡིན། །སྡིག་རྗེས་གཞན་དོན་ཚོགས་གསོག་སྤྱོད་པ་ཡིན། །གཟུང་འཛིན་དབྱིངས་སུ་ཡལ་བ་འབྲས་བུ་ཡིན། །ཡེ་ཤེས་ཕྱོགས་མེད་ཁྱབ་པ་ཡོན་ཏན་ཡིན། །འགྲོ་དོན་ཤུགས་ལ་འགྲུབ་པ་ཕྲིན་ལས་ཡིན། །མིད་དང་བདའ་ལ་དོན་དུ་མ་འཛིན་པར། །མིད་ཆིག་བདའ་ཡིས་མཚོན་པའི་དོན་ལ་སེམས། །ཞེས་གསུངས་སོ། །སྣང་མཁན་གྱི་སེམས་ཉིད་རང་བཞིན་མེད་པས་དེར་བཏགས་པའི་བདག་མེད། སེམས་ཅན་མེད། གང་ཟག་མེད། བྱེད་པ་པོ་མེད། །ཅེས་སོགས། མེད་ཅེས་བྱ་བ་འདི་ཡོད་པར་མ་གྲུབ་པའི་ཐ་ཆིག་གོ །ཡོད་པར་མ་གྲུབ་པའི་ཕྱིར་མེད་པར་ཡང་མ་གྲུབ་པས་མེད་ཅེས་བྱ་བ་འདི་ཡོད་མེད་གང་དབང་མ་གྲུབ་པའི་ཆིག་བླ་དྭགས་སོ། །༈ ཡུལ་རྣམ་པར་རིག་པའི་རྣམ་པར་ཞེས་པ་འདི་ནི་དབང་པོ་ལ་མི་བརྟེན། །ཡུལ་རྣམས་ལས་ཀྱང་མ་འོང་། །བར་གྱི་དབུས་ནའང་མི་གནས། །ནང་ནའང་མེད། །ཕྱི་རོལ་ནའང་མེད། །དེ་བྱུང་བའི་ཆེ་གང་ནས་ཀྱང་མ་འོང་སྟེ། །འགགས་པའི་ཆེ་གང་དུའང་མི་འགྲོ། །དེ་འབྱུང་བའང་སྟོང་། །འཇིག་ན་ཡང་སྟོང་སོགས་གསུངས་སོ། །མདོ་ལས། ཡང་དག་པར་མཐོང་བ་དེ་ལ་ནི་ཆོས་གང་ཡང་སྐྱེ་བར་མི་འགྱུར་ཏེ། ཞེས་སོགས་གསུངས་སོ། །ཡུམ་ལས། ཡིད་ལ་བྱེད་པ་དེ་ནི་འདོད་པའི་ཁམས་དང་། གཟུགས་ཀྱི་ཁམས་དང་། གཟུགས་མེད་པའི་ཁམས་སུ་འདི་བར་འགྱུར་ལ། ཡིད་ལ་མི་བྱེད་པ་ནི་གང་དུ་ཡང་འདི་བར་མི་འགྱུར་རོ། །ཞེས་དང་། མདོ་ལས། གང་གི་ཆོ་ཅི་ལ་ཡང་མི་སྤྱོད་ན། །དེ་ཡི་ཕྱིར་རྣལ་འབྱོར་སྤྱོད་པ་ཞེས་བྱའོ། །ཞེས་དང་། དེས་ན་ཐམས་ལ་ཆོས་མེད་ཀྱི་དང་ལ་སྤྱོད་པ་ནི་ཆོས་

ཀྱི་མཚོག་ཡིན་ཏེ། མདོ་ལས། དེ་ལ་ཆོས་ཀྱི་མཚོག་གང་ཞེ་ན། །གང་
ལ་ཆོས་ཀྱི་འདུ་ཤེས་མེད་པའོ། །ཞེས་སོ། །ཡུམ་ལས། བྱང་ཆུབ་
དམིགས་སུ་མེད་པའི་ཕྱིར་བྱང་ཆུབ་ཅེས་བྱ་བ་འདི་ནི་མིང་ཙམ་དུ་ཟད་དོ། །
སངས་རྒྱས་དམིགས་སུ་མེད་པ་ནི་མིང་ཙམ་དུ་ཟད་དོ། །ཞེས་སོ། །
ཆོས་ཐམས་ཅད་ཀྱི་གནས་ལུགས་ནམ་མཁའ་ལྟ་བུར་རྣམ་ཤེས་དང་ཡེ་ཤེས་ཀྱི་
ཡུལ་དུ་བྱར་མེད་པར་རྟོགས་པ་དེ་ལྟ་བ་ཡིན། དེའི་དང་ལ་མི་གནས་པའི་
ཚུལ་གྱི་གནས་པ་དེ་སྒོམ་པ་ཡིན། རྗེས་ལ་སེམས་ཅན་སྣ་ཚོགས་ཀྱི་དོན་དུ་
བསོད་ནམས་ཀྱི་ཚོགས་སྒྱུ་མ་ལྟ་བུར་གསོག་པ་ནི་སྤྱོད་པ་ཡིན། སྒྱུ་མ་ཙམ་
གྱི་བློ་སྣང་ཡང་དབྱིངས་སུ་ཡལ་བ་ནི་མཐར་ཕྱིན་པའི་འབྲས་བུ་ཡིན་ནོ། །
ཆོས་དབྱིངས་སྟོང་ཉིད་སྒྱུ་བསམ་བརྗོད་ལས་འདས། །ཞེས་བུའི་ཡུལ་ལ་
ཤེས་པ་རང་ཡང་མེད། །མེད་བཞིན་དེ་ཉིད་ལྟ་སྒོམ་བྱེད་པ་ནི། །ནམ་
མཁའ་ནམ་མཁའ་ལྟ་སྒོམ་བྱེད་པ་བཞད། །ཡང་དག་དོན་ལ་སེམས་མེད་
སྣང་བ་མེད། །མེད་པའང་མེད་པས་ཡོད་མེད་རྙེས་ལས་འདས། །
སྟོང་ཉིད་ཟབ་མོའི་དོན་ལ་མི་སྐྲག་ཅིང་རབ་ཏུ་གནས་པར་དགའ་ཞིང་མོས་པའི་
གང་ཟག་དེ་སྟོན་ཡང་ཐོས་ཤིང་སྒྲུབས་པའི་སྐལ་ལྡན་འགྱུར་དུ་བྱང་ཆུབ་ཐོབ་པའི་
རྟགས་ཡིན་པར་བཤད་དོ། །ཆོས་ཉིད་མཁའ་འད་བསམ་དུ་མེད་པའི་
དབྱིངས། །དེ་རྟོགས་ཡེ་ཤེས་བརྗོད་དུ་མེད་པའི་དང་། །ཐིམ་མེད་བྱུ་བུལ་
གཏུག་མ་མཚམས་པ་ཉིད། །འདི་ནི་དུས་གསུམ་རྒྱལ་བའི་དགོངས་པ་
ཡིན། །དོན་དམ་ཆོས་ཉིད་མོ་གཤམ་བུ་འདྲ་ལ། །མི་མཛོན་མི་བསམ་བ
མལ་གཞག་མའི་དང་། །ཀུན་རྫོབ་ཆོས་ཅན་བྱུང་འགུག་སྒྱུ་མ་རྣམས། །མི་
ལེན་མི་འདོར་ཞེན་མེད་ལོངས་སྤྱོད་པ། །རྒྱལ་བའི་དགོངས་པ་རྣམས་སུ་ལེན་
པ་ཡིན། །རྟི་སྲིད་སེམས་ལ་དབང་ཐོབ་མ་གྱུར་པར། །བདག་པའི་ལོངས་

སྟོད་ཀུན་ལ་ཆགས་མེད་ཅིང་། །དེ་དགས་བཞིན་དུ་ཉགས་ཁྲོད་བསྟེན་པ་
ནི། །ཕྱིར་མི་ལྡོག་པའི་ལམ་ལ་གནས་པ་ཡིན། །མཐུན་དང་མི་མཐུན་ཕྱི་
ནང་རྐྱེན་རྣམས་ལ། །དགའ་དང་མི་དགའ་ཆགས་སྡང་ཐོགས་མེད་
ཅིང་། །གང་ཡང་ལམ་གྱི་གྲོགས་སུ་ཆེ་བ་ནི། །སྐྱེ་མེད་ཆོས་ལ་བརྟན་པ་
ཐོབ་པ་ཡིན། །སེམས་ཉིད་མཁའ་ལྟར་རྟོགས་པའི་ཤེས་རབ་དང་། །སྒྱུ་
མའི་སེམས་ཅན་མི་སྡོང་སྙིང་རྗེ་གཉིས། །ཟུང་དུ་འབྲེལ་བའི་ལྷ་སྟོད་
མཆོང་ལྡན་པ། །མི་གནས་ཡེ་ཤེས་ཆེན་པོར་མྱུར་ཐོབ་
འགྱུར། ༈ མྱང་འདས་ལས། སྟོང་པ་བུ་བ་ནི་སྟོང་པ་དང་མི་སྟོང་པ་
ཉིས་ཀ་མི་མཐོང་བའོ། །སྟོང་པའི་རང་གདངས་ཅིར་ཡང་སྣང་ཞིང་། །
སྣང་དུས་ཉིད་ནས་སྟོང་པས་སྣང་སྟོང་ཟུང་འཇུག །དེ་ཀ་རང་གིས་ཁ་ནང་དུ་
ཕྱོགས་ཏེ་རིག་པར་བྱ་བ་ལས་གཞན་མ་ཡིན་པ་སོ་སོ་རང་རིག་ཡེ་ཤེས་སྟོང་ཡུལ་
བ་ཞེས་སོ། །མ་ཚིག་གིས། གང་ཡང་ཡིད་ལ་མ་བྱས་ན། །ཀོལ་བར་
འབྱུང་བ་ག་ལ་ཡོད། །འདུ་ཤེས་རྣམ་པར་བཞིགས་ལ་ཞོག །ཅེས་དང་། །
སེམས་ལ་གཉིས་སུ་མ་མཆིས་པས། །བཀླ་ཀྲུ་མེད་པའི་ཚུལ་དུ་བཞུ། །
བཅུས་པས་རང་གི་སེམས་མི་མཐོང་། །མཐོང་བས་སེམས་ཉིད་དོན་མི་
རིག །དེ་བས་བཀླ་བར་བྱ་བ་ནི། །ཐུལ་ཙམ་ཡོད་པ་མ་ཡིན་ནོ། །ཞེས་
སོ། །སེམས་ཉིད་སྟོང་གསལ་དམིགས་མེད་གཞིས་ཀྱི་གནས་ལུགས་ཡང་
དག་པའོ། །རིག་པ་སྒྲོས་བྲལ་དོས་བཟུང་མེད་པ་དེ་ཀ་འཆར་སྒོ་མ་འགགས་
པའི་རྩལ་སྤྲུང་སྣ་ཚོགས་སུ་ལྷ་བྱུང་ཞར་བས་མཚམས་བཞག་དང་རྗེས་ཐོབ་དབྱེར་མེད་
དམ་འབྱུང་འཇུག་གསལ་སྟོང་འཛིན་མེད་ཀྱི་རང་དུ་ལ་བློ་བར་བྱས་ཏེ་ཉམས་སུ་
བླང་ངོ་། །ཞེས་སོ།།

INDEX

actuality ... 1, 5, 7, 11, 15, 21, 27, 34
actuality of knowables in general 1
actuality of the rational mind 5
actuality of their knower itself 1
affliction 21
afflictions 5, 33
agent producing the appearance 10
arrogance and conceit ... 5, 6
authentically looks at the authentic itself 8
awareness 3-6, 21-23, 25, 32, 37, 40
becoming 11, 22, 24
beyond expressions of speech and thought 12
bodhichitta 22, 26
bodhisatva . xx, 1, 4, 6, 22, 26, 38
bodhisatvas on the tenth level 1
clinging ...... xv, 2, 3, 13, 22
complete liberation 8
complexion 14, 23
confused appearance 5
confused awareness 4
confusion ...... xiii, 4, 22, 23
consciousness .... xviii, 5, 10, 11, 22-24, 29, 31, 32, 39
conventions 3
correct fictional .. xii, xiii, 2, 4
cross over 15, 24
dharmadhātu 2-4, 6, 7, 9, 12, 24
dharmadhātu free of all elaborations 6
dharmadhātu free of elaboration 2, 12
dharmatā 5, 6, 13, 24
dharmin 25
dhātu . 2-4, 6, 7, 9, 12, 13, 24, 25
direct perception . 2, 3, 27, 29
discursive thought 8, 25
divided two truths 4
division into two truths .. 4, 5

dream-like, illusion-like
   sentient beings 8
Dza Patrul . 1, i, iii, v-ix, xx, 1
Dzachuka v
Dzogchen .... vi, vii, 32
Dzogchen Monastery .. vi, vii
elaboration .... xx, 2, 4, 7, 12,
                           15, 25
elaboration-free actuality of
   knowables 7
elaboration-free actuality of
   the knower 7
enlightenment mind   8, 22, 26
Entering the Bodhisatva's
   Conduct 4, 6
entity 2, 26
equipoise 8, 15
equipoise empty of both
   knower and knowables .. 8
Essence Mahāmudrā xxi
expressions 12, 27
fact .... vii, xiv, xvii, xx, 7, 10,
   12, 13, 23, 27-30, 33, 37-39
fictional ... xi-xiv, xvii, xix, xx,
            1-6, 9, 13, 27, 28
fictional and superfactual
   .... xiv, 28
fictional rational mind 6
finality obtained 28
first to tenth levels 2
fortunate person 28
free of all extremes 4
freedom from elaboration
   .... xx, 2, 4, 25
full internal comprehension
   .... 4, 5
generic image 3, 9, 29

gradual-style practice 8, 9
grasped-grasping 9, 29
grasping at things 2
Great Completion . vi, viii, ix,
   xxi, 23, 24, 26, 32, 33, 36-
                          38, 42
Great Middle Way 5
Great Vehicle .. 1, i, iii, v, viii,
                 1, 26, 30, 31
ground 7, 30, 34
Guardian Maitreya 8
habituation 30, 31
higher level of arrogance ... 6
Highest Continuum 8
identification 7, 15, 31
immediate-style practice ... 8
incorrect and correct fictional
   .... xii, 2
incorrect fictional ... xii, xiii, 2
individualized beings 3
indivisible two truths .. 4, 5, 7
inference 3
innate ... 2, 4, 7, 9, 13, 15, 31
inseparable appearance-
   emptiness 5
intent 31
intentional conduct 2, 31
Jigmey Chokyi Wangpo   v, vii
Jigmey Lingpa vi
Kagyu .... v, 32, 42
knower .. 1, 5, 7, 8, 12, 21, 32,
                       36, 40
knowledge of the two truth's
   characteristics 7
latencies 2, 32
latency 32
like uncompounded space .. 7

INDEX

liveliness 15, 33
Longchen Nyingthig vi
Longchen Rabjam vi
loving-kindness and
   compassion 8
luminosity or illumination 33
luminous-empty rigpa 7
Mahāmudrā . . . xxi, 23, 24, 26, 32, 36-38
māra 6, 33
mental mind 2, 5, 34
mentation 11, 14, 34
mere appearance 2, 3
merely illusory enlightenment mind 8
merely illusory two accumulations 9
mind . vi, xi, xii, xvii, xviii, xx, 2, 4-10, 12, 13, 15, 21-40
mindness 7, 10, 14, 15, 34
Nirvāṇa Sutra 14
noble one 28, 34
non-referencing 37
non-regressing 35
Nyingma . . . . v, xv, 32, 42
Other Emptiness . . . . . xxi, 35
overstatement 35
paramārtha 38, 39
paramārthasatya 39
post-meditation xx, 1, 8, 11, 15
prajñā 3, 4, 14, 35, 36
preserve 8, 11, 36
profound realization 9
Quintessence . . . vi, viii, ix, xxi
Quintessence Great Completion . vi, viii, ix, xxi
rational mind 4-6, 9, 12, 23, 36
rational mind is the fictional 6
realization vi, 2, 5, 7-9, 11, 36
reference and referencing . 37
relative and absolute 28
rigpa 7, 15, 22, 29, 33, 37
saṃsāra . . 9, 22, 25, 28, 33, 39
saṃvṛtti 27, 28
saṃvṛttisatya 28
satva and sattva 22, 38
scent of musk 2
self-knowing direct perception
   3
sense faculties 10
sense of a personal self 5
shine forth 8, 38
space-like 5, 8, 11, 13, 14
space-like actuality of all dharmas 11
state . . xx, 8, 9, 11, 13, 15, 22, 26, 30, 36, 38
superfact dharmadhātu 3
superfact which is one's own nature 2
superfactual . . . xi-xiv, xx, 1, 2, 4, 6, 28, 38, 39
superfactual truth xi-xiii, xx, 39
the actuality of knowables in general 1
the actuality of the knower itself 5
the authentic . . . 8, 10, 12, 39
the dharma that will be practised 8
the dharma to be realized . . 1
the domain of rational mind 6
the fictional xii, xiii, 1-6, 9, 13
the four mind-reversers . . . 9

the gradual-style practice for those with duller faculties 9
the great freedom from elaboration 4
the immediate-style practice for those with sharp faculties 8
the *Mother* 4, 11
the provisional realization .. 5
the superfactual 1, 2, 4, 6
The Sūtra Petitioned by Kāshyapa 6
The Sūtra Petitioned by Maitreya 7
the ultimate realization .. 5, 7
things and non-things 4
third turning .. xxi, 11, 26, 35
Thorough Cut .... ix, xiii, xx, 28, 37
those of duller faculties 8
those with sharp faculties ... 8
two truths .... 1, i, iii, v, viii-x, xii, xiii, xv, xviii-xx, 1, 3-9, 13

two truths have three modes of appearance 3
Shāntideva 4, 6
ultimate dharmadhātu 4
ultimate indivisible two truths 5, 7
ultimate presentation xx
ultimate two truths .... xiii, 4
unsatisfactoriness 39, 40
vast prayers of aspiration ... 9
wisdom .... viii, 5, 10, 11, 13, 14, 22-24, 27, 31, 32, 34, 35, 37, 39, 40
wisdom of non-dual dharmatā 5
without realizer and realized 7
without referencing . 4, 11, 15
without seer and seen 7
words and symbols of communication 10
work of māra 6
wrong awareness 6

www.ingramcontent.com/pod-product-compliance
Lightning Source LLC
Chambersburg PA
CBHW031638160426
43196CB00006B/467